Vegas and the Mob

Al W Moe

ALSO BY AL W MOE

Nevada's Golden Age of Gambling

Stealing From Bandits

The Roots of Reno

Mob City: Reno

Getting Thin is Murder

TABLE OF CONTENTS

INTRODUCTION

"Oh, What a Tangled Web We Weave."

Most people have a romanticized image of the Mob and Las Vegas floating around in their head. They think of the movie *The Godfather* and imagine the Mob came to Las Vegas, a few people were shot, and then the FBI came along and straightened everything out. Nothing could be further from the truth! In addition to great staying power, the Mob was very concerned about their image in Nevada and went to great lengths to make sure that when they had to whack somebody, it was done out of town, but it was still done, regularly.

If you want to think of a movie to personify the Mob's pre-Las Vegas activity, think of *The Departed*. That's right, remember when Leonardo DeCaprio was bent over a pool table having his already-broken arm beaten with a heavy boot? That's more like the way it was. There were no nice guys and every day was life and death. Tough guys beat, tortured, and killed their competitors, and sometimes moved up in the family hierarchy. When they did, the heads of other families tried to kill them. Often, they were successful. And then along came Las Vegas, a place in the sun.

The Mob had a strong grip on Las Vegas by the time the Kefauver Committee came along in 1951 and spilled the beans that mobsters owned casinos in Nevada. Sure, there had been suspicion, but TV viewers were still shocked by what they heard and saw. They would have been even more shocked to learn that the FBI already knew what was being discussed on TV because they had been tapping phones in Vegas for almost ten years, but they never shared their information. So, with all the new-found knowledge, did anything change? Not really.

The Mob ruled the casinos and the politicians, and the public went warily along with their gambling, hoping they were safe. They knew that "Bugsy" Siegel once said, "We only kill our own," so they watched over their shoulder and hoped for the best. It was exciting. Siegel, as you may have heard, made a name for himself long before he came to Nevada, and it wasn't for selling bubble gum.

During Prohibition in the 1920s, every person with a bathtub could make gin, and every person with a whistle to wet could get a drink at a local speakeasy. It was a sign of the times, like flappers, prosperity, and the Ford Model T automobile, because nine out of every ten cars sold were Fords. By the same token, nine out of every ten illegal casinos were paying juice to the local gang, and the Sheriff, and the councilmen, and the mayor, and sometimes there wasn't much left for the operator, but then something wonderful happened, Nevada legalized gaming.

Although gambling was as easy to find as bootleg whiskey in Nevada, games of chance had to be housed "out of view" of passerby on the streets. Casinos flourished in basements and second story lofts, but in 1930, a 29-year old Republican State Assemblyman named Phil Tobin used a failed 1929 bill for the legalization of gambling and presented it to his fellow politicians. This time they were interested. The Great Depression was crushing Nevada's few legal businesses, and the state was about to collapse within its borders.

Passage seemed more certain this time, but just to make sure everything went right for the "sporting men," as the illegal casino owners liked to call themselves, Reno's George Wingfield and Bill "Cinch" Graham rained money down on the politicians like confetti. The bill passed the Nevada State Assembly and the Senate easily, and Governor Fred Balzar signed the bill into law on March 19, 1931. Casinos were legally taking player's money before the ink could dry.

The Northern Club in Las Vegas got its gaming permit the next day from the Sheriff's Department. Owners Morgan and Stocker celebrated their legal status with free drinks at the bar until the regular evening crowd came in, then it was business, and drink prices, as usual. You could still get a good cigar for a nickel, or soda pop.

Whiskey at the bar was a dime. The six slot machines in the corner were nickel and dime varieties. The casino offered a tub-style crap game and a roulette wheel. If you wanted to play poker, there were tables near the bar, where the air was continually filled with a haze of blue smoke that the belt-driven fans could do little to disperse. The skim of Las Vegas casino profits was soon to come.

The Boulder Club and Las Vegas Club were licensed a week later. Bugsy Siegel would someday have an office in the Las Vegas Club where the FBI secretly listened to every phone call but did nothing to stop the flow of Vegas cash to Meyer Lansky and his Mob associates. What a great country!

Away from the confines of downtown, the Meadows in Meadow Acres and the Pair-O-Dice out on Highway 91 were licensed during the summer. The Meadows was run by Los Angeles bootlegger Tony "The Hat" Cornero and his brother, who had supplied, and been made rich, by several Mob families. The new club was described by the *Las Vegas Age* newspaper as, "Potent in its charm, mysterious in its fascination, the Meadows, America's most luxurious casino, will open its door's tonight and formally embark upon a career which all liberal minded persons in the West will watch closely."

Apparently, not-so-liberal minded people on the east coast were also watching closely. "Lucky" Luciano (November 24, 1897, Lercara Friddi, Sicily, Italy) helped bankroll Cornero's bootlegging operations and wanted a piece of the pie. He sent Meyer Lansky to investigate, who found the resort to be quite delightful, with carpeting, polished tile, and a tight little casino with roulette tables, craps, faro, chuck-a-luck, and slot machines. The players were rubes, lacking in gaming skill. The money was good.

Lansky relayed the news that Luciano expected 25 percent off the top. Cornero refused and sent Meyer on his way. He didn't get mad; he got even. The next week a fire burned down the casino. Cornero and his brother burned a hole in the highway back to California and stayed away for 15 years.

1 PROHIBITION RICHES

The casinos of Nevada were watched closely by gangs in Detroit, Kansas City, Minneapolis, and Toledo. In New York, Charles Luciano had his own casinos but told associate Meyer Lansky to compare the casinos in Nevada to his operations in the Big Apple and those in Kentucky. In Chicago, Al Capone was already familiar with Bill Graham's clubs in Reno and knew Graham was available for money laundering through his casinos and George Wingfield's Riverside Bank. The Reno group had already handled hundreds of thousands in bogus stock deals and was willing to help Alvin Karpis and Ma Barker's gang when they needed to launder ransom money from their kidnappings.

When they did, the gang members would hang around the Rex and Bank Clubs, drinking slowly, and sometimes losing most of what they came to launder after Graham took his 15 percent fee. A year later, "Pretty Boy" Floyd was in town, followed quickly by "Baby Face" Nelson, whom Graham set up with a home just a few blocks from his own. Reno was cozy.

Capone didn't care much about the Reno clubs in the 1930s because his casinos in Chicago produced more income than any clubs in Nevada did, and besides, he was the King of Bootlegging, so he didn't watch too closely. He should have been watching the government, and Elliot Ness, who had a serious infatuation with capturing Capone doing something illegal that he could charge him with. There were some informants and witnesses, but they kept having accidents and disappearing. None ever testified in court. Eventually, Ness and a team of accountants managed to get Capone convicted of tax evasion in 1931.

Capone may have been well-known and as tough as they come, but his future had prison written in big letters. He appointed Frank Nitti to run his operations, who immediately held a summit where Paul Ricca was promoted to Underboss and second-in-command when enforcing the Outfit's law. Tony "Joe Batters" Accardo, who didn't get his nickname because he liked baseball, was promoted to "capo" or captain, in charge of enforcement. At the same time, Charlie Fischetti took control of the nightclubs and gambling casinos, which operated openly with the cooperation of the police, who looked the other way as long as they got their weekly payoffs.

After that, time ticked slowly for Capone, and it would be a decade before Accardo was in charge, ready to muscle in on the action in Las Vegas and Reno.

Meanwhile, Capone got sentenced to 11 years imprisonment, even after bribing witnesses and paying off the entire jury (the judge had to switch juries from one courtroom to another). Although he got easy time at the Atlanta U.S. Penitentiary with special privileges and was able to assert some control over the Chicago gang, Alcatraz loomed in the foggy distance. He got sent to the Rock on August 11, 1934, losing contact with his criminal colleagues, and joining the general populace at the formidable prison as just another dogface with a number.

Capone learned in his first week at the Rock that his social standing had fallen dramatically and forever. He got a standard cell, no privileges, and after shoving his way to the front of the line for a haircut, Capone was cornered by fellow prisoner James Lucas, who met him eye-to-eye and told him, "Get the hell to the back of the line." Capone thrust out his chin and asked Lucas if he knew who he was, to which Lucas replied, "Yeah, I know who you are, grease ball. And if you don't get back to the end of that fucking line, I'm gonna' know who you were." Capone walked off without his dignity or a haircut.

Luciano had his own trouble over the years with close shaves, but usually avoided the worst of what the city had to offer. Born November 24, 1897, he grew up fast and tough and was knocking around the streets of New York at 15 after he quit his $5 a week gig as a shipping clerk. He didn't like the Irish thugs in the neighborhood who terrorized the Jewish kids, so he met a few of them with a crowbar and beat them until the others understood he was as serious as a steamroller. After that, he offered protection to Jewish kids in Brooklyn for 10-cents a week. He met Meyer Lansky (born July 4, 1902) at a fellow hood's office and liked him immediately. He was slightly built, but "Didn't take guff from nobody," and he already had a buddy bodyguard named Benjamin Siegel.

Siegel was born in the Williamsburg district of Brooklyn on February 28th, 1906. He never finished grammar school because he was too busy rolling drunks and burglarizing empty lofts with the other neighborhood punks. By the age of 12, he was pulling stickups with his older teenage friends. When prohibition got to be the biggest moneymaker the government ever thought up to make the underworld rich, Ben, like so many others, got involved in a more "organized" pursuit of cash. He worked for whoever had the best action.

The first gang, headed by Luciano and run by Albert Anastasia, would be around even after the Kefauver hearings into organized crime and gambling in America during the 1950s. The second gang was an all-Jewish group that Ben and Meyer belonged to, started soon after Ben met Meyer at a street craps game he was running. Two gangs wanted the lucrative spot outside a candy store for their crap game, and boys being boys, well, a knife was pulled, then a gun. During the scuffle the gun hit the hard pavement, so did one of the gang members. A beat cop down the street headed over to investigate.

Ben scrambled on his knees for the piece, but the older Meyer snatched it from his grip. As they ran from the scene amid police whistles, Ben yelled, "I need that gun." Meyer shook his head and thrust it into his overcoat. When they were blocks away and safe from the heat, Meyer was able to reason with the hyperactive kid about why he was keeping the revolver. Over the years, it was Meyer, and Meyer alone, who was able to look into the crazed, menacing eyes of "Bugsy" Siegel and make him understand.

The US Government enacted the Volstead Act on January 15, 1920, to save us all from the sins of drink, and once-legal breweries and distilleries were out of business, some for weeks. Others closed down, but the brew was still available whether it came from a local warehouse or across the water from Canada. Prohibition put every tough, enterprising criminal in the country into business. The likes of Al Capone could never have amassed their fortunes without the government's help. With the tremendous income produced, politicians became so many pawns in the running of gang-controlled cities. Gangs and gangsters ruled the streets, took over entire cities and were nearly impossible to stop.

Joe Masseria was The Man in Brooklyn. Bosses rose and fell in relation to the power they wielded, the money they produced, and the ruthlessness of their rivals. In 1921, Masseria was the *don* of Brooklyn and reported to no one. He enlisted his most trusted partner as his business advisor, or consigliere, and recruited gunmen like Luciano to join his crew. He needed plenty of help against the other gangs in New York, and Luciano already had powerful ties to other mobsters. Luciano was also close to New York's biggest "high finance" gambling entrepreneur, Arnold Rothstein.

Rothstein was a sporting man, and he liked big scores, like throwing the 1919 World Series. He set the standard for payoffs with thousands of dollars a week going to union heads, police units, and all the way to Tammany Hall. He constantly shielded himself from the illegal acts of graft and bribery with buffer-after-buffer and put his good–producers to work scoring easy money in rackets like protection for local shop owners of up to fifteen percent of what the thugs thought the stores were producing in revenue and loansharking.

One of those "producers" was Frank Costello, another was Charlie Luciano, and still another was Meyer Lansky. Meyer brought Siegel along as his number one man. Moe Sedway, a tiny hood with big fish eyes and a square nose, also went to work for the gang.

Rothstein helped give Luciano some class by teaching him some manners and taking him to his tailor so that he could dress more conventionally, but still flashy enough to be noticed as a big spender. When Luciano botched a drug deal, Rothstein introduced him to bribery, telling him, "Buy 200 tickets to the Jack Dempsey–Luis Firpo prize fight at the Polo Grounds in the Bronx and spread'em around to the local politicians and gang bosses," and it helped.

Luciano learned that the bigger the wheel, the more grease it took to keep it moving away from him. Within in two years, Luciano's gang was grossing a million dollars a month. His bootlegging operation moved into Philadelphia and New Jersey, and he used Ben Siegel as a button man when needed because Siegel didn't mind doing the hitting.

Rival gangs didn't care much for newcomers moving in, but a few cracked heads or the murder of a gang's leader kept Ben and Meyer on top. Siegel was tagged with "Bug" or "Bugsy" for his maniacal behavior, and he was making more money than he could spend. Big dinners, dames, cigars, and new duds were now the standard. He had all of his clothes tailored: silk shirts with long collar points, pinstripe suits, fancy leather shoes he had buffed at a shoe-shine stand twice a day, and long jackets with fur collars. He liked to wear his Fedora tilted slightly to the right, giving him a more menacing look.

When he wasn't casing a joint or forcing himself on a woman who had refused his advances, he was into bookmaking, bootlegging, hijacking, extortion, and loan sharking. Whatever paid the most and offered the best action, that was for Bugsy. He took his lumps, but always gave back twice what he got. When he was picked up for questioning by the police and had a black eye, they knew someone else was dead.

Another of the tough guys in the 1920s was Davie Berman, who liked to blow up post offices. He was hot with dynamite, and let nobody stand in his way. He was experienced with bank jobs and had a crew that could handle the exchange of checks and writs for cash. And, he liked to do the occasional kidnapping. In May of '27, armed with machine guns, hand grenades, and tear bombs, he and three other thugs went in search of Abraham Scharlin, a local bootlegger. Scharlin was just the type of guy the gang liked to kidnap. Who could he complain to?

Scharlin was snatched off the street as he walked to his car and held in Brooklyn while a $20,000 ransom demand went to his partners. All this at a time when a new car was $500, a house was $1200, and a beautiful steak dinner with all the trimmings was under a buck! Scharlin's partners stalled, just long enough for the police to recognize Berman, wanted by postal authorities, standing outside a haberdashery on West 66th Street with fellow kidnapper Joseph Marcus.

Their descriptions were called in, and two NYPD detectives rushed them with guns drawn. Marcus drew his pistol and was shot dead, Berman, his head whipped with a blackjack, hit the pavement and was out cold.

Berman was taken to a local precinct but refused to tell investigators anything about his business associates. When the kidnapping made the *Daily News*, it called his crime "The most sinister plan of a gigantic kidnapping trust whose activities are aimed at underworld overlords." For two days Berman was refused food or sleep and beaten to a pulp, but he had turned to stone. His only comment was, "Hell, the worst I can get is life." It was enough to send the police into fits of rage, and people in speakeasies all over New York are repeating the phrase, which was quoted in the paper. Berman landed in Sing Sing Prison, but he never did "sing."

Arnold Rothstein always paid good money and was safe from the police, but he was killed in 1928 while trying to collect a $51,000 poker debt from George "Hump" McManus. In an interesting twist, the three-day game had been rigged by Alvin Clarence Thomas (Titanic Thompson), and Rothstein was trying to collect from McManus because he had to pay $319,000 from the shellacking he had taken in the game. He died before learning his poker skills were still good; he had been cheated. McManus was charged but found innocent of the killing. Later, Dutch Schultz took credit for the killing of Rothstein.

With his mentor gone, Luciano joined forces again with Masseria, but there was no love lost, and neither trusted the other. Also, rival gang boss Salvatore Maranzano was pushing into Masseria's turf. Each time a neighborhood was taken, another dead body was found in an alley, a car, or a bathroom. When you got hit, you hit back; it was the law of the land. Bugsy preferred two shots in the head, one in the chest.

The resulting Castellammarese War left dead bodies all over the city, often two and three a day. Dozens and dozens of gangsters were found beaten, stabbed, and shot. Luciano was determined to form a local group of allied crime families, but his idea didn't sit well with Masseria.

In October 1929, three gunmen forced Luciano into a limousine where he got pistol-whipped, stabbed a dozen times, and dumped for dead on a beach at Staten Island. When the tide went out, Luciano was still alive, earning himself the nickname "Lucky." The attackers left him with some vicious zipper scars and a droopy eye, but the beating cemented his conviction that there had to be a meeting of the families.

At the same time, Nevada was legalizing gaming; Luciano was organizing his moves. On April 15, 1931, Luciano and Masseria had lunch in a Coney Island restaurant. The veal was excellent; the wine, fair. Luciano excused himself and went to the restroom while his most trusted button men, Ben Siegel, Vito Genovese, Albert Anastasia, and Joe Adonis strolled into the restaurant. They walked up to Masseria, took out their guns, and blasted away until the air was filled with smoke. The other diners, the cook, the owner, and the waiter saw nothing.

Maranzano was now safe, happy with Masseria gone, and set about dividing the Italian-American gangs in New York City into the Five Families. Each family was headed by a trusted man, starting with Maranzano himself. The other four families included Gagliano, Luciano, Mangano, and Profaci, and each man was the family's *don*. Now the *dons* could meet to discuss grievances, and each family was treated as an equal, able to make their own money, so long as it didn't interfere with each other's turf. Of course, Maranzano was more equal than the others, declaring that he would be Capo Di Tutti Capi, the top boss of all the families. And then he got greedy, taking bits and pieces of the other family's lines of income.

Meanwhile, since even gangsters have family plans, Meyer and Ben went on with normal lives behind the murders. Meyer (born in Grozny, Russia) became a naturalized citizen of the United States in 1928 and was married. Ben too, was seeing someone, well, lots of someone's, but a family was a good idea, so he took up with Esta, the sister of a friend and fellow killer Whitey Krakower. They were married in 1929 and Ben bought her a new car and a house in Scarsdale, but she didn't drive, Bugsy got her a driver. Then, the partners who founded what became known as Murder, Inc. had children and led married lives, but they weren't nine-to-five guys.

Hits continued, and Lansky, Siegel, and even Luciano were regularly arrested. In three years Bugsy was picked up for questioning 11 times. Once he had to pay a $50 fine. Siegel was a known killer who farmed his services out to other families and locations for heavy work. He took at least two trips to Chicago to fill contract killings. No job was too tough for him, and he never failed to complete a contract.

When their boss, Maranzano, felt threatened by Luciano, he had him arrested (one of 25 arrests without a day in jail). When that didn't work, Maranzano sent Vinnie "Mad Dog" Coll to get rid of him, but Luciano, lucky again, was tipped off. In September of '31, Luciano sent his gang of shooters to head off the attack. Posing as government agents, they busted into Maranzano's office, guns drawn and took his bodyguard's revolvers. Then two of the "agents" stabbed Maranzano repeatedly before shooting him. They let the bodyguards go.

Later, two button-men caught up with Mad Dog in a five-and –

dime. When he finished his sandwich at the counter and went into a phone booth, two hoods used Chicago-style force, and his body was nearly cut in half with blasts from a Tommy-gun. Dutch Schultz took credit for the hit on Coll.

A few weeks later, Ben had another of his manic episodes. He was busy setting up a new casino and speakeasy in a downstairs alleyway location of Manhattan when two goons dropped a large, heavy box that contained a roulette wheel. The lid flew off; the wheel skittered to the ground, and a large crack on the side was obvious.

They had skirted around Ben, afraid to ask him to move, and the result was the loss of a $185 wheel. Ben kicked the closest man and shouted, "You idiot, that's your pay for the month," and when the second man opened his mouth in protest, Ben pulled out his gun and smashed it against his ear. Blood spurted across the floor as he fell and Ben continued beating him until he stopped moving. He was dead.

Any slight or backtalk had to be met with action, and any reproach from a rival had to be met head-on in Bugsy's World. When Waxy Gordon wouldn't share two of his gaming joints in New York with Ben and Meyer, they paid off an IRS agent to look at his income and Gordon was indicted for tax evasion.

In retaliation, Gordon sent his lieutenant, Charlie "Chink" Sherman and Andy and Louie Frabrazzo to kill his rivals. The two men risked their lives lowering a bomb down the chimney of the Hard Tack Social Club at 547 Grand Avenue in New York City. Designed to kill Siegel and Lansky, the bomb got stuck in a right-angle offset that stopped the device from reaching the correct elevation.

The bomb did explode, sending wood, bricks, and metal sheeting down into the social club. Siegel and two other gang members ended up in the hospital. Debris from the blast left Bugsy with cuts that required stitches, including one from a flying brick that ran two jagged inches along the left side of his head. It was clearly visible after that and burns from the blast left him hot for revenge.

Meyer put a dozen button men on the street, and they found Andy Frabrazzo hiding out in Jersey. The police found Andy the next week, stuffed into a sack on a deserted lot. His knees, feet, and hands were all smashed, and his teeth knocked out. The following month, his partner, Louie, met a barrage of bullets in Manhattan. A brother, Tony, wasn't involved with setting the bomb, but he figured the best defense was a good offense, so he took to writing his memoirs.

The law of silence, or Omerta, was sacred to most mobsters, and Bugsy, was no exception. In September of 1932, Ben checked himself into a hospital with stomach cramps. That evening he slipped out of his room, went down the fire escape, and picked-up two trigger men. They drove to a small, poorly lit home where they posed as detectives to entice Tony Frabrazzo to come out onto the stoop, leaving his sausage and spaghetti behind in the kitchen. With his parents standing in the background, Bugsy came out of the shadows and filled the remaining brother with lead. He had his revenge, and he headed back to the hospital unnoticed, but changes were coming.

With Luciano's main rivals dead, he abolished the title of Capo Di Tutti Capi but elevated his Italian associates to new positions in his crime family. Joe Adonis, Anthony Carfano, Michael Coppola, and Anthony Strolla were each *made men*, and now caporegimes. Ben was a trusted associate, but wild, and he was drawing too much heat. For everyone's sake, he would have to leave New York soon. Lansky was a most trusted financial whiz who had already begun using new techniques for hiding the spoils of the Mob's enterprises, but he, like Ben, wasn't Italian, and killer or not, could not be *made man*. Only those with long family lines back to the old country that could be traced and threatened if necessary could be *made men*.

Luciano kept the Five Families the way they were, but Vito Genovese was promoted to Underboss, and Frank Costello became the Luciano Family consigliere. It was time to go national.

2 LUCIANO TAKES CONTROL

The Commission was designed to settle all national disputes over territories and businesses. First composed of the Five Families of New York, it grew to include the crime families of Buffalo, Philadelphia, Detroit, Kansas City, Chicago, St. Louis, Milwaukee, and eventually Los Angeles. Miami was an open city, so was Las Vegas. The plan was to quietly control all the major crime and mobsters in the United States and share the wealth to a small degree, in a fair manner.

At the very first meeting of the heads of the families, it was agreed that Luciano would indeed preside over the negotiations and that

Lansky would provide financial planning when asked. It was also agreed that Benjamin Siegel would be going to Los Angeles, and Jack Dragna would share the West Coast's gaming profits with New York, and Chicago. And, profits would soon be coming from Minneapolis, too.

Seven and a half years after going stone mute, Dave Berman walked out of Sing-Sing prison a free man. He never "ratted out his partners," and they were grateful. The week he got out of prison he took up with Moe Sedway and joined the floating crap game at 8th Avenue and 15th Street run by Joe Adonis. Dinner guests that week included Meyer Lansky and Albert Anastasia; Berman was again a part of Murder, Inc., but it was now late 1934, and New York Mayor Fiorello La Guardia was ruining the good thing the Mob had. Every month, barges filled with slot machines were being hauled out to sea and dumped. It was a disaster. It was also a good time to look elsewhere for greener pastures, or at least green felt for gambling tables, to exploit the masses with.

Berman was rewarded for his time in prison with a handful of cash. Frank Costello presented the money in an open safe, and Dave was told, "Whatever you need, Dave." Berman, a "stand-up guy" till the end, asked only for a small sack of cash to get back to Minneapolis with, where his brother "Chickie" had set up some local gambling and race booking while he was in Sing Sing. He also asked permission to run Minneapolis for the group's gambling interests. Permission was granted.

At the same time in Chicago, 17-year-old Virginia Hill (born 26 August 1916) took a waitress job at the San Carlo Italian Village, a popular spot with the Capone gang. She was a terrible waitress, but oh, the legs she had! Joey Epstein, the accountant for Jake "Greasy Thumb" Guzik, took a shine to the fresh-faced kid. He told her boss to find another dame, and off they went to the track, where he used her as a front to bet a few steamers (winning horses in rigged fields). Later, he introduced her to Major Arterburn Riddle, a local trucking company tycoon the Chicago Outfit kept happy so he would front for them in various enterprises. Riddle fell immediately in lust with Hill and bought her a mink coat and a diamond necklace. She could be had, regularly, but she couldn't be bought and owned.

When she gained Epstein's trust, Hill worked as a money handler, transporting suitcases of cash from one enterprise to another and from illegal enterprises to legal ones to be laundered. Virginia also became a plaything for the bosses, livening up the Fischetti Christmas party and passed around the table like hard candy; she performed fellatio on every boss in the room after wishing them a Merry Christmas. What-a-gal.

In New York, Dutch Schultz had legal problems. Out of the blue, there was some strait-cat government guy that couldn't be bought. The horror! The man was U.S. Special Prosecutor, Thomas E. Dewey, and he was taking his job very seriously. Schultz was arrested for tax evasion, making his numbers racket vulnerable to the Luciano Family. Dutch appeared before The Commission and demanded that he be allowed to kill Dewey. Permission was denied.

Schultz, furious about the denial, accused The Commission of siding with Luciano so he could take over his businesses and promised to kill Dewey anyway. Members met again later without Schultz and agreed that the effect on their enterprises would be catastrophic if Dewey had an accident. The only way to avoid the fallout would be to kill Schultz instead. The task was given to Albert Anastasia, and he picked Louis "Lepke" Buchalter to handle the dirty work.

On October 23, 1935, Schultz went to a meeting with his accountant and two bodyguards at the Palace Chophouse at 12 East Park Street in Newark, New Jersey. It was a quiet place, good veal chops. After lying low for months and staying out of the papers, Dutch was happy to be out.

When dinner was finished, Schultz hit the restroom, and Charles Workman hit him, with a gunshot to the chest. The Dutchman went down immediately. Two other shots missed him, but Workman was a thinking killer and had soaked his bullets in water for days, making them rusty, so even if the bullets didn't kill Shultz, he would develop peritonitis. Workman moved out of the bathroom and into the restaurant where he joined his partner, Emanuel Weiss, who was unloading his shotgun at the rest of Schultz's party.

All three men, Otto Berman (no relation to Dave Berman), Abe Landau, and Bernard Rosencrantz were hit with lead buckshot; Landau also caught a bullet through the aorta from Workman's gun.

Landau and Rosencrantz both crumpled to the ground but returned fire, and Workman and Weiss high-tailed it for the door. Landau grunted, got to his feet, and followed them outside, emptying his gun before collapsing against a trash can.

Back inside, Rosencrantz staggered to the bar and demanded nickels for the pay phone. The bartender stood reluctantly from behind the bar, snapped open the cash register, and spilled a handful of nickels on the bar. Rosencrantz struggled to the phone booth, got the operator, and ordered an ambulance before staring at his shoes, filled with his blood. He then collapsed inside the booth.

Outside, an ambulance siren shrilled from far away. When the medics arrived, they assumed Rosencrantz was dead from his slumped position with his head down and nearly touching the floor, but he spoke two words, "Lotta blood." He and Landau were whisked to the nearest hospital because they were in the worst shape. Police refused to let either man go into surgery before spilling the details of the shootout, but neither man spoke. Eventually, the doctors prevailed, and the men went under the knife.

Berman and Schultz were in desperate shape by the time the second ambulance arrived. The Dutchman, refusing to die in the john, crawled twenty feet into the restaurant and propped himself up against a booth. He was still lucid when the new medics attended to him, and he thrust a stack of $100 bills at them, "To make the trip fast and fruitful," he said. The ride was quick, the surgery long, and unsuccessful. Dutch Schultz died the following afternoon.

Although The Commission and Lucky Luciano had saved Thomas E. Dewey's life, Luciano's luck ran out in 1936 when the same Mr. Dewey arrested him for his role in a massive prostitution ring. On July 18, 1936, Luciano was sentenced to from 30 to 50 years in state prison, and taken to Sing Sing.

Before he wore stripes, Luciano conferred with his Underboss, Vito Genovese, about running the crews, and The Commission. Less than two months later Genovese was indicted for murder and fled the country to Naples, Italy. At that point, his consigliere, Frank Costello, took temporary control of all business aspects of Luciano's empire. When Luciano's final appeal to the United States Supreme Court was refused in 1938, he stepped down, and Costello assumed permanent control.

Costello was all for expansion of the Mob's empire and was happy to have income from sources outside New York. Lansky flew to Florida and then on to Cuba, where the family was running two casinos at Oriental Park. Lou Smith was fronting the racetrack and casinos for Fulgencio Batista, but they were struggling financially and had a bad name. Enter Superhero Meyer Lansky to the rescue. He brought his own crew of supervisors to administer the table games, and Al Levy of the Down Town Merchants Club ran the crap games for Meyer. The casinos immediately turned profitable with the play from the few local businessmen with deep pockets and vacationers from the US. Meanwhile, with politics as usual in Cuba, virtually no taxes (and of course no kickbacks) were making their way back to the general populace who continued to live in slum-like conditions.

Through all the racketeering, the prostitution, and the current legal machinations, gambling was bringing in a larger and larger share of revenues for the Mob, with casinos in New York, New Jersey, and Florida. Also, Lansky and Luciano had engineered deals in Kentucky and Hot Springs, Arkansas, and those clubs were beginning to prosper.

In Cleveland, the Mayfield Road Gang, headed by Moe Dalitz, was doing very well, and Costello wasn't the only one watching. The FBI was watching too, and regarded Dalitz's Thomas Club and Ohio Villa to be, "Swank night clubs, both notorious gambling resorts located near Cleveland in Cuyahoga County, Ohio."

The 1939 memorandum for the director of the FBI, John Edgar Hoover, noted that both of Dalitz's clubs had been, "Entirely renovated in order to provide additional space and facilities for its patrons, including the installation of a cooling system at the Durham Road location of the Thomas Club, Maple Heights, Ohio."

Hoover's memo continued, pointing out that, "Moe Davis (Dalitz) has been indicated as a close and intimate associate of Louis Buchalter. This same gang is said to be in control of gambling, policy and other rackets in Cuyahoga and adjacent counties and other cities, including Miami, Florida, where the Frolics Club is operated during the winter season. Thomas McGinty is another member of the "Cleveland Syndicate" who owns a gambling casino in Miami,

Florida, named Carter's Casino, and the Fairgrounds Race Track in New Orleans, Louisiana.

The FBI was also keeping close tabs on Bugsy Siegel, noting in memos that he was moving about the city in a bulletproof limousine and kept an apartment at the Waldorf Astoria Towers, two floors above the one Lucky Luciano used to have. He was constantly traveling, taking in Florida, Acapulco, and Hot Springs, Arkansas, and he was dining with George Raft and a bevy of starlets in Hollywood, including Jean Harlow, who was having an affair with Longie Zwillman (head of New Jersey's crime family).

When the heat was too much in New York, Bugsy moved his family to Los Angeles so he could move in on the gaming and racketeering that the burgeoning city offered. Mickey Cohen became Siegel's chief lieutenant, and while Dragna was willing to cut the East Coast group and Chicago in for some of the profits, he wasn't too happy that Siegel immediately dispatched lookouts with high-powered binoculars to steal the race results at local horse race tracks to past-post his bookies and collect on races that were already finished. Some partner.

Meanwhile, Siegel's wife, Esta, and their daughters, Millicent and Barbara, had trouble adjusting to California, even though their godmother was Jean Harlow. Bugsy did not. He was right at home in Beverly Hills and began hobnobbing with movie stars and filmmakers. He handled a hit for the Chicago Outfit, and then drove to Las Vegas to meet a few connected friends at the Northern Club in downtown Las Vegas.

The Northern had received the first Nevada gaming license, issued to Mayme Stocker, on March 20, 1931. By this date, the Stockers were simply leasing out the gaming concession to a nice little fellow from New York, a Mr. Moe Sedway.

3 THE FALL OF DOWNTOWN

Las Vegas never had a chance to be a regular city. It may have been founded by the greatest salt-of-the-earth guys who ever walked the planet, but that's not who wound up owning it.

A hundred years before the legalization of open gambling it was little more than a small oasis of grassland along the Old Spanish Trail. By the turn of the century, when the land had worked its way through the hands of several owners, the San Pedro, Los Angeles & Salt Lake Railroad Co. bought 1800 acres to develop the Las Vegas town site and sell parcels of land to support the train stop. Ever wonder how the railroad owner's got rich?

In 1928, the town consisted of just 5,100 hearty souls. They weren't men and women of vision; they were just trying to make a living on the face of the sun. There was no air conditioning, and the summers ran to 118 degrees. Who would live in such a hellhole? Where were the farms, the greenery, and the money?

The town did get an indoor theater in '28, and they called it the El Portal, built on the site of the old Las Vegas Airdrome, which was a movie in an open field. It opened on June 21, and tickets were a hefty twenty cents each. The show was a pre-release screening of Clara Bow's movie "Ladies of the Mob." How prophetic! Clara liked to play roulette at the Cal-Neva Lodge at Lake Tahoe, but she didn't like to pay when she lost. More than once she left bum checks at the cashier's cage, they totaled $10,500 in 1932.

The train stop at the end of Fremont Street in Las Vegas was like those in other towns along the railroad lines. You know, greasy spoon diners, seedy hotels, dice games in the shadows, cheap prostitution. Something for everyone stepping off that hot, dusty train, until it was time to build Boulder Dam. Then local officials had to try and rein in the illegal drinking and prostitution, which of course was impossible. They settled for a scrubbing of the downtown area to make it more palatable to inspectors from Washington.

The dam site, about 25 miles from Las Vegas, attracted every skilled laborer and out of work bum within 2,000 miles, and nearly overnight there were 20,000 men loitering around the town and planned worksite. 5,000 lucky ones got work; the rest migrated on to California where they went to work in Hollywood. Alright, that might not be true, but they left because Las Vegas wasn't a place to hang out if you didn't have a job. At least not until the 1970s when you could get a breakfast special for ninety-nine cents and all the drinks you wanted for free by just wandering around the slot machines in the local casinos.

Work began on the dam in March of '31, within days of the legalization of open gaming. Soon, the monthly construction payroll of more than $500,000 was being siphoned off the blackjack and craps tables by the friendly casino owners of downtown Las Vegas. The workers stayed broke; the casino bosses got rich, and Fremont Street got the first traffic light in Las Vegas in 1931. And, as a show of appreciation and trust that the future was good, the street was finally paved, although it would be another six years before the bulk of Highway 91 to Los Angeles was paved.

On April 1, 1931, the Boulder Club opened at 118 E. Fremont Street. Aptly named, the club was organized by half-dozen partners: Joe and Jack Murphy, Clyde Hatch, Walt Watson, "Pros" Goumond and A. B. Witcher. They called it "The best casino by a dam site." They also kept their profits.

Jim Young came to Las Vegas in 1932 as a skilled poker player and faro dealer. And, because strange things happen in Vegas, he managed to earn enough money at $15 a day dealer wagers to buy part of the Boulder Club, and then the Silver Club, around the corner at 108 N. 1st Street. Although there was no bar, Joe Morgan's Golden Camel Bar was next door, so pretty soon the liquor flowed through a swinging door, and the casino's fortunes increased greatly.

In fact, the club was so valuable that Young had to pay for it twice. With the onset of World War II, Jim hoped for enrollment in Officer's Candidate School. To allow him time away from the club, he struck a deal with Joe Morgan next door, who had purchased his license in 1938 and ran two 21 games, a tub craps game, and four slot machines. He was more than happy to look after the Silver Club for Jim Young.

When Young didn't get into OCS, he came back to Las Vegas and what he considered "his club." Unfortunately, since his deal had been that he would be back after the war, Morgan refused to give up the Silver Club, and Jim had to buy it again, but he wasn't forced to share his profits with the Mob. Not yet.

Once the dam was built, the whole damn future of Las Vegas looked bleak. The town had grown considerably. There were businesses, churches, general stores, and the train that noisy train kept bringing people to town, but things were stalled.

As the 1930s closed, Bugsy Siegel was busy extorting the Hollywood unions, setting up a supply of drugs from Mexico for the Chicago Outfit, and shuttling to Vegas on the occasional weekend to check with Moe Sedway. Moe was running things at the Las Vegas Club, the El Cortez, and the Golden Nugget. He was a whiz at finding other people's money and spending it. It takes a lot of cash to buy houses, cars, politicians, police officers, and especially police chiefs. Plus, all those trips to Mexico, to San Francisco, that year-round suite at the St. Francis, the hotels in Hollywood and Beverly Hills. It was as much work to spend it as it was to steal it.

Meyer Lansky wasn't working nearly as hard. He was getting "skim" money, the cream of the profits, from casinos all over the country, not just the legal ones in Las Vegas. And, he shared; distributing the bulk of it to New York, but Detroit, Philadelphia, and Kansas City were getting a taste too. In Chicago, Tony Accardo had his thinking cap on; it was time to get more from Vegas, and Reno, too.

Late in 1939, Bugsy went to a party at George Raft's house. At the bar, Raft introduced him to a tall, redheaded woman with a quick wit and a smart mouth. Bugsy was flummoxed for one of the few times in his life. The next day he met her at the Beverly Wilshire hotel where she introduced him more closely to her smart mouth.

The following day, Siegel and his brother-in-law, Whitey Krakower, met with Frankie Carbo and Allie "Tick Tock" Tannenbaum. They talked, smoking a pack of Lucky Strikes between them, and then drove out to see their old friend, Harry "Big Greenie" Greenberg. Harry was a hitter, like them, and he'd been there to say goodbye to both Louis and Andy Frabrazzo when Bugsy needed his help. Now, "Big Greenie" wanted the Bug's help after stirring up a hornet's nest by demanding money from Louis Buchalter.

Greenberg was happy to see Bugsy, and Siegel was happy to see him too, because old friend or not, he hated squealers, even those like Greenberg who just threatened to squeal. So, instead of a happy reunion, Greenberg got whacked. For the local press, it was another day at the office; gangland slayings were common in L.A. with criminals taking advantage of narcotics, prostitution, bookmaking, and gambling to fill their coffers. With that many vices, some toes were going to get stepped on, and some heads, too.

Siegel fit right in, and he made sure everyone knew he was in charge. At a business meeting to discuss his terms (it's my way, all the way, and 25 percent), local loan shark and bookie Les Brunemann asked, "Are you fuckin' kiddin' me?" Bugsy wasn't. A month later Brunemann was shot three times at the Roost Café in Redondo Beach, his own turf. He recovered, but he wasn't any smarter than the last time he asked Bugsy a question. He went to dinner in the same restaurant, this time catching seven bullets. It was his last meal.

In between the shootings, Siegel's thugs, armed with pistols and tire chains, raided every bookie joint they could find and took over the bookmaking in Redondo Beach. Then, they worked their way up and down the coast, forcing deals from backroom casinos, poker parlors, and even the local dog and horse tracks.

When Bugsy was strong enough in Southern California with a big enough gang, he met Tony Cornero and demanded a larger cut of the profits he was making with the SS REX. Why not? His gambling boat anchored strategically 3.1 miles off the coast of Santa Monica (three miles to international waters and no gambling ban at the time) were doing great. Each night little skip boats (water taxis) took players out to the ship, and with all the money in Los Angeles, Cornero was getting rich. Bugsy got what an increase. Vegas was hardly on his mind.

When Bugsy did travel to Las Vegas, his cut from the El Cortez and the Golden Nugget was already in the safe at the Las Vegas Club when he arrived. What a business. The three clubs did less than his clubs in Los Angeles, San Diego, or Mexico, where he had a vested interest in several casinos like the Agua Caliente, but it was steady and easy, and legal. Maybe there was something there after all.

Also, Mexico was trying to shut down gambling, so was California. The Mob's infiltration of Las Vegas had been surprisingly easy. Bugsy and Moe Sedway simply found a club they liked, met with the owner, and said, "Geez, you guys need to fix up your casino. You need more crap games and 21; you'll need some cash to do that. We'll help you out."

Not a single casino owner ever refused to take a little cash from Bugsy in exchange for a piece of the action. Siegel was a known commodity, and you can't say no to a guy who's killed more people than he can remember. Usually, Siegel stated 30 percent, but took 55 percent of the profits, with 25 percent going to Meyer Lansky.

After the first club had fallen into the Mob's hands it was like dominoes; they just keep going down. It was like potato chips or women. Once you had one, you couldn't stop. If the owners squawked, they were told, "stay home and the boys will handle everything." The "owners" could come in once a week and get their remaining breadcrumbs. Downtown fell without a gunshot, but not without a few guns in the ear.

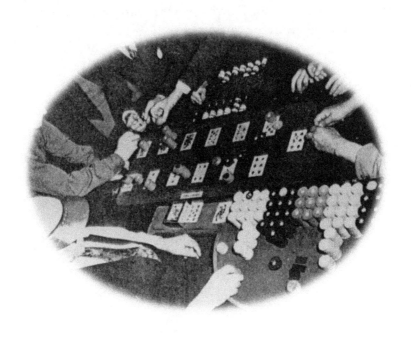

4 SIN CITY EXPANDS

The El Rancho Vegas broke ground in 1940 on Highway 91 to Los Angeles after local businessman James Cashman convinced Thomas Hull, the owner of the El Rancho hotel chain, to build a resort in Las Vegas. It wasn't because they envisioned a great line of hotel casinos, it was because the land was cheap, and besides, there was no space left downtown. Hull didn't have to bargain much with Mrs. Jessie Hunt, who owned the 33 acres of sand and sage; she only asked for $150 an acre. Her husband had paid $10.

Located at 2500 Las Vegas Boulevard, at the southwest corner of Las Vegas Boulevard and Sahara, the club opened on April 3, 1941, with 110 rooms. It was a welcome sight for those hot, drenched, and weary travelers along the highway from Barstow, and a temporary new home for those who came from towns like Steubenville, Ohio or Covington, Kentucky to run the new casinos in Las Vegas.

It wasn't fancy with its western-style cowboy theme, not by Hollywood standards, but still ran a hefty $500,000 to build. Extra water was pumped into the area so the grass would grow and a large swimming pool proved quite inviting. Inside, the Opera House theater brought locals and visitors alike a classy show every night. The casino was almost an afterthought, with just two 21 tables, one roulette table, one crap game, and 70 slot machines. The gaming concession was leased out to a couple of fellows with ties to the Cleveland and New York families who offered to take care of the tedious task of counting the money. Nobody bitched.

In 1941, Siegel was arrested by the FBI on charges of harboring a fugitive, Louie "Lepke" Buchalter. Bugsy was livid that one of his former hitters, Abe Reles, had "dropped a dime" on Buchalter and the Greenberg hit. In truth, the FBI knew more than they were admitting to because Reles sang like a bird. All about Bugsy, and about Frankie Carbo, and Buchalter, and he told in vivid detail about his exploits along the way to 14 Mob hits. And, he was ready to testify in open court that most of those hits were done at the behest of one Benjamin Bugsy Siegel.

Now Bugsy needed Reles hit, but the D.A.'s office was watching over him day and night. They moved him from town to town, and for 20 months Reles was held under guard consisting of six police officers. Fortunately, money makes the world go around, and while the charges were still pending, Abe Reles fell from the fifth-floor window of his room at the Half Moon Hotel in Coney Island. The door was locked and guarded by a local officer. Without a witness, the FBI's case dissolved.

In Vegas, life went on. The second hotel-casino on the Los Angeles Highway opened just up the street from the El Rancho. Called the Last Frontier, the property had previously been the Pair-O-Dice. Most recently the hotel was owned and operated by Guy McAfee, a retired Los Angeles Police Captain (oh, how much money the Vice Squad can make you!) who thought it would be a fancy club that could cater to the Southern California trade. A great idea, but he never got a casino going, so for $35,000 he sold the property and facilities to R.E. Griffith. Griffith was connected to the El Rancho Hotel group and owned the property in Gallup, New Mexico.

Griffith couldn't wait to show up the El Rancho with a unique and superior property, but he was delusional; his property didn't turn out different at all. It was a cowboy town setting in a second-rate town in the middle of nowhere. It was desert, it was hot, it was Las Vegas, and it was tough to get built with the Second World War going on.

The obtaining of material was an adventure in patience, persistence, and ingenuity. Bribe money helped too. Especially when it came to wiring and electrical supplies, but the contractors were resourceful. They went out and bought old mines in Northern Nevada so they could strip the materials and reuse them. They also had to buy farmland to grow enough crops to feed the new guests who were coming to town. And last, but not least, they had to find someone to run the casino. Now, who could that be?

Within a year, Thomas Hull sold his points in the El Rancho to Moe Dalitz and Meyer Lansky. The new owners of record for the Clark County gaming license, Hilton-Brown, worked fine as a front, for a while, but they kept wanting to be in the count room when the table game drop boxes were opened and the money was counted. The nerve of some guys. The Mob needed a guy who knew the score, a guy with more ego, and less greed, and that man was Wilbur Clark.

Wilbur had been in Reno recently, trying to run his own club (the Bonanza) at 207 N. Center Street, just down from the Bank Club. It was a money-loser. There was no way to compete with Bill Graham's Bank Club two doors down, so when he got back to Vegas, he put his remaining cash (about $35,000) into the old Northern casino downtown, fronted for the Mob, and kept his mouth shut. The name changed to the Turf Club; it wasn't his idea. Then he took the head front man job at the El Rancho, too.

Vegas casinos weren't big yet, but they got some big money play on a regular enough basis and were profitable. Billy Wilkerson, Nick "The Greek" Dandalos, and a host of others weren't shy about losing

$50,000 on the weekend. Of course, Nick always got in more hours playing than the others did.

The Greek was fanatical about gambling; it was his whole life. He played for hours on end in a never-ending orgy of bets. One such event started when he put in 40 hours playing Faro Bank at the Golden Nugget while yelling at the dealers, pinching the cocktail servers, and losing his usual tack. But that wasn't enough. After losing $16,000 he got tossed on his ear when he started a fight with the casino manager, but instead of calling it quits, Nick hustled up Glitter Gulch to the Boulder Club. The sawdust joint was in full swing, but Nick only cared about the gamble the place provided, and he bellied up to a jammed craps game and splashed his remaining bankroll on the layout.

Nick beat plenty of men over the years with his superior math skills and some savory sleight-of-hand, but those vices didn't help him any at the craps table. Jim Young, a partner in the club, watched the game closely for hours before taking a turn dealing. He went to breakfast and returned to see Dandalos energized and surrounded by a sea of chips. The hours passed.

Eventually, high tide gave way to low as the Greek's chips dwindled and his luck started to stink up the harbor. The ride was over. Jim Young headed out the door in search of some shut-eye. The Greek, well, he probably searched all day for someone to teach his craps system to, for a price so that he could get back in action.

While the two casinos out on Highway 91 were doing good business, they weren't any busier than the clubs downtown. The casinos were mostly grind joints that catered to locals and the town's few visitors. So, every club had to have a lively race book. And, to run a race book they had to have access to the wire, which gave them constant updates on jockey changes, scratches, and final race results from the race tracks across the country.

For that information, the Continental Press Service had a monopoly, and James Ragen didn't want any partners, but Tony Accardo in Chicago wasn't happy being shut out of the profits, and neither were the boys in New York. They resented Ragen getting $100 a week from every bookie in the states, and when they couldn't buy their way in, they set up the Trans America race wire to compete directly with him, with Bugsy Siegel as the lead salesman.

Mickey Cohen traveled with Siegel, explaining the principles of the new wire: buy or die. Most bookies paid in cash, quickly. As a young man, Mickey had been a prize fighter, and when there was trouble with a bookie refusing to pay for the new wire service, Cohen was likely to go a few rounds with the guy's head. Nobody refused twice.

At night, Cohen sometimes got lucky with the women rejected by the handsome and now polished Siegel, who only slept with the classy dames he met in bars. Mickey, not much of a talker and built like a stocky fireplug, needed all the help he could get.

In Vegas, Moe Sedway got every casino race book in town to sign up. He never needed to call Siegel or Cohen for help. Within a year, Siegel's end of the business was a hefty $25,000 a week. When that wasn't enough, he simply borrowed money from a Hollywood movie mogul or star and never paid them back. Two studio bosses gave the friendly Mr. Siegel over $100,000, and so did film star George Raft, who followed the mobster around town like a puppy dog. Hollywood was perfect for Bugsy; Vegas was a hole. He hated making the trip into town to get his share of the profits, but he was feeling some heat in L.A.

In late 1944 there was too much heat for Davie Berman at his Minneapolis clubs, too. Political change was coming, and Las Vegas looked good. He called Frank Costello and Meyer Lansky and asked about taking his cash to the legal desert town. As a token of his esteem, he put up $160,000 front money to Meyer for permission to buy into the El Cortez and head the group running it. The Commission granted permission.

Berman brought his brother Chickie, and upon arriving in Las Vegas for the purchase, Dave went to see Sedway first. Chickie held the second cash payment in a satchel, but only for the evening. Sometime between 8:00 p.m. and 11:00 p.m. he managed to find a crap game with high enough limits to blow through several hundred thousand dollars. Davie found him dazed and crying in his room. He packed up and jumped into a car with Chickie and drove out of state.

News travels fast, and so do mobsters who think they've been burned. Before Davie got back to Minneapolis, his partners had put out two contracts on Chickie's life. Mistakes were mistakes, but business was business. Berman had just enough cash and enough remaining friends to cover the Minneapolis group's investment. A week later, Davie called in the rest of his IOU's to keep his brother alive, and on May 10th, 1945, Davie turned over the cash himself to Meyer Lansky.

The new owners of the El Cortez were Dave Berman, Meyer Lansky, Willie Alderman, Charles Chickie Berman, Moe Sedway, Gus Greenbaum and Ben Siegel. The gaming license remained the same as it was from 1941 until January of 1949. Money was split between the owners, and a weekly satchel of cash went directly to Lansky, whether he was in Las Vegas, Miami, or New York. Lansky handled the skim for every group claiming a piece of the pie. By then it was clear they had mint pie.

The casinos downtown were small, but they were now air-cooled and offered 21 and craps for as little as ten cents, and keno too. Chuck-a-luck and roulette could be played for twenty-five cents, and if the player wanted a "color" at roulette, the chips were available for five cents each. There were even penny slots. The most popular slot machines were nickels, but table games and the race book got the most action. Many clubs also had a poker table or two, but there were always a few players who were allowed to bet much higher stakes, even if the stated limits only went as high as fifty dollars.

At the El Cortez, Willie Alderman kept a jaundiced eye on the dealers. If someone was out of line, he set 'em straight. Willie got his nickname in Minneapolis, and it wasn't because he liked chopped ice in his drinks. Willie "Ice Pick" Alderman wasn't somebody to mess with. If you saw him joining you at the bar, it was already too late. He liked to sidle up to a man and plunge an ice pick through his ear and deep into his brain. As the dying man slumped to the bar, Willie would say, "Poor guy can't hold his liquor." Next, he would wrap a long arm around him and muscle him to a handy laundry chute or a car waiting in the alley.

As for the table games, they were straight. Players were able to enjoy their gambling, knowing they wouldn't be cheated. Unless of course they won too much or got drunk. Drunk patrons stood no chance of getting out of the casino with any cash. Players that won too much were still treated well, but "coolers" were brought in to adjust the odds a bit. That was tough at roulette and craps, but at 21 a mechanic dealer would deal "seconds" (the second card from the top, saving the top card for the dealer's hand) when they had to, to make a winning hand for the house.

If a player got belligerent while winning, a pit boss might just look at the bar, get the tender's eye, and slowly smile while rubbing his nose. Then, the next drink for the player was a "Mickey Finn," and the player would quickly become incapacitated by chloral hydrate. A trusted source says certain pit bosses and bartenders had a running bet on whether the player passed out on the table, or fell off their chair. The pit boss got a buck for passed out players; the bartender got five dollars if the player fell off their chair. Occasionally the player broke their nose in the fall, but these things happen.

Over the next three years, Davie Berman worked the El Cortez, the Las Vegas Club and the El Dorado. As the pit manager, he took an 11 percent cut of the combined take. Siegel owned 25 percent, and Greenbaum and Alderman each had 10 percent. The skim was constant, a 25 percent rake off the top for the bosses back east. Cocktail servers started wearing short dresses and taking drinks to the tables. Cigarette girls sold "cigars, cigarettes, Tiparillos," and showgirls were required to stay after the dinner crowd left the showroom for at least an hour.

Many hung around the bar in skimpy costumes that accentuated their curves and could easily be talked into taking a look at a player's hotel room, for say, five dollars. Bellmen and valet attendants took to offering male and even female visitors a companion for the evening for only a slightly higher price. Ah, what Las Vegas could offer!

Gus Greenbaum was a Phoenix bookie in the 1940s who contracted with Siegel and paid him a weekly fee. When Siegel called Gus to tell him he was arranging a new wire service (Trans America) and to do the physical set up for him in Phoenix and Tucson, Greenbaum was resistant. He said, "There's already a service here, and dat's too much competition, Ben." Siegel replied, "Don't worry Gus, I'm going to be out there next week to see you, and I'll personally straighten this out." Gus had a change of heart. Later, he was happy to go to work for the likes of top boss Frank Costello at the El Cortez in Las Vegas. Costello still worked for Luciano, in Italy.

Dave Berman, now in his early 40s, was self-educated, personable, and had been a war hero. He took to being called Davie, even by new associates. He simply wanted to work in his casinos and spend time with his wife and child. His daughter, Susan, never suspected that her father was connected to the underworld. She saw him only as a loving father, who worked long hours at his hotels. Her mother had already seen too much, she spent most of her time confined to a sick bed at home or a Los Angeles psych ward, and passed away at a young age.

In the gambling community of the 1940s and 1950s, many of the Las Vegas bosses had criminal backgrounds. However, they were drawn by Nevada's tolerant atmosphere. If a large investor could not get licensed or wished to stay off the official papers, then a front man was used. How bad could that be?

When Kay Starr played the casino for the first time, she thought she had to gamble, as well as sing. She tried craps, loused up the game for the other players, and lost her first night's salary.

Davie Berman strolled over and told her, "Stay away from the tables. How can you make people happy with your singing if you know you owe us your whole salary because of your gambling?" In Vegas, he was just a boss looking out for the best interests of his boss (Costello), his casino, and his family. In that order, of course.

Lucky Luciano was inventive, even from prison, and with enough whispers in the right ears, he convinced the U.S. Office of Naval Intelligence in 1942 that Albert Anastasia, who controlled the docks in New York, that he could make a great impact on the war effort. He guaranteed there would be no strikes in New York harbor, and that contacts in Italy would make the US involvement much safer.

His contribution was minimal, but it still translated to release from prison. Luciano was taken to Ellis Island and then a freighter in Brooklyn harbor. On February 9, 1946, he was allowed a spaghetti dinner with Albert Anastasia and five guests. In the morning, the freighter sailed to Naples. Luciano set up the Mob business in new offices, then flew to Cuba, to take over The Commission once again.

5 THE FLAMINGO

William "Billy" Wilkerson (born September 29, 1890), was a well-known restaurateur with Southern California hot-spots like Ciro's and La Rue. He was also the managing editor and owner of the Hollywood Reporter. He worked and worked, and then he played and played. In fact, Billy was compulsively compulsive. He drank as many as twenty Cokes in the afternoon, and smoked like a demon; he stayed up all night and never gave it a thought. When it came to nightlife, he *was* the nightlife. The compulsive businessman hit the horse track every day, kept a pair of dice in his coat pocket, and found casinos in L.A., San Diego, and Las Vegas that could handle his heavy action.

When the action wasn't enough, he decided to buy himself a casino, so he leased the El Rancho Vegas for six months, paying $50,000. Wilkerson figured if he were busy running a casino, he wouldn't have time to gamble, but he was wrong. He still played at the Last Frontier and the El Cortez.

Two months into his lease he saw a "For Sale" sign on a plot of land along the road back to Los Angeles. It was a couple of miles from the Last Frontier, but maybe building his own casino would do the trick. Las Vegas hadn't managed to attract much in the way of a Hollywood crowd yet, and although casinos as far away as Elko were paying for big-name acts, the clubs in Vegas weren't. The wheels in his mind went round and round

They spun at a fever pitch for weeks until he slowed them down enough to make some phone calls, and in late January of 1945, Wilkerson purchased a 33-acre parcel of land owned by Margaret M. Folsom for $84,000. It was much more than the land was worth, but money was no object at the time, and he started designing his hotel and casino with a Hollywood flair. He hired designers; he hired architects; he would have hired a big brass band if Las Vegas had one, and by the time the finishing touches were in his design the property was slated for two hundred rooms, as many as the El Rancho and Last Frontier combined. In the center of the building, the plans showed a large casino that every patron, whether coming in to dine, or to get a room, would have to walk through.

Branching off from the casino was everything a guest could want: fancy restaurants, a huge showroom, the hotel, and of course, air conditioning. He planned on spending another $1.2 million. He had $200,000 on loan from Howard Hughes and convinced Bank of America to loan him $600,000. To make up the $400,000 difference he took to the gambling tables and lost.

To get more cash, Wilkerson drove downtown and pitched a deal to Gus Greenbaum and Moe Sedway. Would they run the casino for him and give him a cash advance? Of course, they would, and they gave him more credit to play at the El Cortez. By the end of the year, Wilkerson owed Moe Sedway $400,000 and was broke. Construction came to a dead stop, and his building sat baking in the sun. For two months he shuttled back and forth between L.A. and Vegas, always stopping to walk the construction site with his architect and discuss what could be done if they just had more cash. During one of those walks a sleek Buick pulled up, and a Mr. G. Harry Rothberg from the East Coast emerged from the car.

He walked slowly across the sand, scanning the lot, and then introduced himself to Wilkerson. It didn't take much encouragement for Billy to show Mr. Rothberg his building plans. He was intrigued. He talked about the design, the total square footage, whether the cost could be kept under $12 a square foot. They connected. They laughed. They got down to brass tacks.

Rothberg asked how much Billy needed to finish, and off the top of his head Wilkerson said, "A million dollars." In exchange for financing, Rothberg took two-thirds ownership but promised no interference. A contract was signed, and the money arrived at Wilkerson's bank. The sun rose, the birds sang, construction started again, and then Greenbaum and Sedway arrived one day with Rothberg's (and now Wilkerson's) managing partner, Bugsy Siegel.

Things went from bad to worse for Wilkerson as the months dragged on. Bugsy had always hated the heat of Las Vegas, perhaps a little sun stroke was to blame, but at some point during the summer, Siegel truly snapped. By then he had already gone through the million that Costello contributed via Lansky and he was so busy changing plans and annoying the architects every moment of the day that his relationship with Virginia Hill was sinking fast. They spent most of their time glaring at each other in the midst of angry discussions, then running off to their room to work out the kinks. Workers steered clear of them, and Wilkerson watched his control over the project wither away.

When Virginia just wouldn't stay quiet about the interior decorating, Siegel drove downtown to what he considered a haven from the noise. In the quiet of his office at the Las Vegas Club, Bugsy and his head henchman, Moe Sedway, were able to chat. They discussed the race wire plans, designs for the Flamingo, and ways of getting enough cash to complete the new project. Everything they said was picked up on microphones and wiretaps placed by the FBI, which, continued on its steady course of doing nothing and not rocking the boat.

Under continuing money woes, Bugsy flew to the Midwest twice, then to New York, collecting $600,000 in cash and a lot of concerned looks. Meyer gave him the same advice as the last time he showed up wanting money, "Ben, stop fussing with the features and get the joint open," but the Flamingo had swallowed him up.

He wanted full control and pressured Wilkerson to take corporate stock in exchange for five percent more ownership. Wilkerson could read the writing in the sand and give in. Now with full control, Bugsy put Virginia in charge of the interior decorating. Accordingly, she blew through the money like wind through a fishing net. She also took a trip to Paris and on to Switzerland, where she deposited some "emergency" money in a numbered account.

About the same time, Bugsy's wife, Estelle, or Esta, was in Reno, "taking the cure," (establishing six-week residency) and waiting for a divorce. Siegel had no issues with the idea. Their lawyers agreed to $600 a month in alimony and $350 a week for child support. You read that right, about $2100 a month in 1940s money. Yowza!

The next month Siegel insisted that Wilkerson sells him the land, and they agreed on five percent more stock for half the land, but Siegel was relentless. The more he got, the more he wanted. Six weeks later he got the remaining land for another five percent, making Wilkerson a 48 percent partner, but not in Mob parlance. In June of 1946, Benny formed the Nevada Project Corporation of California, and of course named himself president. Wilkerson was toast. That's when the FBI finally decided to chime in.

J. Edgar noticed that the Chicago Outfit was expanding, so the FBI started Capga (Capone gang). It was a deep investigation into what they considered a resurgence of the old Al Capone gang in Chicago, the wire service, and what they saw as a new interest in Las Vegas from The Commission and gangs in Cleveland, Detroit, and New York. Hoover told the United States Attorney General the situation was "Out of control, almost epidemic proportions," and he needed approval for more wiretaps as well as microphone surveillance on Meyer Lansky and Bugsy Siegel in Los Angeles and Las Vegas, and not just their home phones. The Attorney General agreed and turned the FBI loose to tap all residences, hotels, and places of business used by Siegel and his associates.

When the FBI had more information on the Flamingo deal, J.

Edgar Hoover himself got in touch with Wilkerson to tell him that his partner, Mr. Siegel, was a dangerous character and he might want to be careful or extricate himself from the project. Wilkerson was candid with J. Edgar, "It's too late," he said.

To put pressure on Siegel and the Mob, Hoover leaked a story to Walter Winchell about a West Coast racketeer who was attempting to muscle a prominent West Coast newspaper publisher out of his interest in a hotel project. Winchell immediately took it live via his radio broadcast on July 14, 1946. His announcement went nationwide, and it was almost his last. It didn't take a genius to figure out who the story was about.

When friends told Winchell it was Siegel and Billy Wilkerson, both of whom he knew, he started sweating bullets. He made phone calls; he wrote letters, and he met with Wilkerson personally and babbled in his ear until he agreed to write a letter to Siegel. Eventually, his groveling was enough to keep Bugsy from killing him. Since they were friends, he caught a break, once he admitted that Hoover was his source, and only because Siegel kept calling Moe Sedway in Vegas to see if there was any scuttlebutt on the street about the broadcast. There wasn't. Nobody in Vegas cared.

A phone call between Virginia Hill and Siegel got recorded by the FBI from Siegel's room at the Last Frontier. Bugsy said, "I'll get him (Winchell) to make the Director meet with me, and I'll make that cock sucker tell me how he got the info, and I'll kill the people who gave it. If this makes it so I can't get a license here, what am I going to do with the hotel, stick it up my ass? I'll knock his fucking eyes out." On August 5, 1946, the first gaming license for the Flamingo was denied by the Clark County Commissioner's office.

Siegel was frantic to get more cash, but he wasn't making any friends with the delayed opening, and he wasn't able to get more capital without showing a license. He put another $62,500 into the construction himself, asking Meyer to do the same. Lansky agreed, forwarding a check, but told him, "Ben," the well's dry. Get the club open. It was never designed to be a $2 million front." If only that were all Bugsy had spent.

Siegel agreed, knowing there was no way to get any more cash from his bosses, but he did ask for one more favor, according to FBI notes. "Meyer, I need a carload of beer," he said, before hanging up the phone.

The carload wasn't a couple of cases of suds; it was a full railroad boxcar load. Meyer got in touch with Arthur H. Samish, who represented the California State Brewers Institute. No problem. Alfred Hart Distilleries, of Los Angeles, California shipped the boxcar of beer via rail into Las Vegas. Siegel offered it directly, to at least get his liquor license. It was granted the following week.

With all the FBI had, they didn't feel they had enough. They were working the investigation into Capga and Siegel out of the Salt Lake City office, where three agents were assigned to the case. An additional officer was working full time in the Los Angeles office, and other agents were contributing to the investigation, including a new Las Vegas Resident agent. They were also looking into allegations of bribery involving several politicians, including Senator McCarran of Nevada.

Materials were hard to get in the postwar market, but Siegel learned early how to buy friends. He had US Senator Pat McCarran rearrange priority lists to allow the Flamingo to get many of the metals and fixtures unavailable to other builders. Even wood, steel, and electrical conduit and wiring were in short supply, but whatever was needed, McCarran could get. The price was still no object.

Siegel carried two notebooks with him at all times. He constantly wrote notes about costs, delivery schedules, doodles that were his encrypted financing ledgers, and he noted problems with workers and subcontractors, who to hit later. He was precise and meticulous. If the numbers didn't come out right, he'd fly into a rage. If the amount quoted by a contractor varied, he refused to pay. The problem was if it matched, he did pay, when he had the cash, even if the original estimate had been way too high.

After a week in Los Angeles scraping together what cash was available from his narcotics deals and his bookie's joints, Bugsy returned to Las Vegas in the fading sunlight and checked on the progress of the Flamingo. It was coming together, starting to look like a resort. He went up to the third floor where the penthouse, his penthouse, was being finished. There was no door yet, and the bulletproof windows hadn't been delivered yet, but it was shaping up.

When he walked into the main room, he cracked his head on a support beam, too low for him to walk under. He pulled out his handkerchief and mopped his brow. There was blood, and he certainly saw red. He ran downstairs to find a working phone line and called his lawyer, Lou Wiener, and yelled at him for five solid minutes. Lou drove from his office to the work site and joined Bugsy upstairs. At five-feet-six-inches, he was able to walk under the beam; he didn't see what the problem was and told Bugsy so. Bugsy didn't think it was funny at all.

Siegel spent another five minutes yelling at Wiener, then ten minutes screaming at the architect. In the end, he accepted that the design he had personally okayed included the beam. Removing the beam and redesigning roof supports ran a pricey $78,000, nearly everything Bugsy had brought back from California. His project was a giant hole in the ground sucking him dry, and still, things got worse.

A front-page story in the Las Vegas paper criticized the construction of the Flamingo when materials were badly needed by veterans for the construction of homes. Prompted by the newspaper story, the Civil Production Administration (CPA) put a "Stop Order" on the entire project and instructed Siegel and his architect to meet with the directors at the CPA West Coast office in San Francisco in October.

The original plans approved in January were for a single building. By March, Siegel had visions of grandeur, and the project was changed to three building. He had completely changed the entire project and was caught with his hand in the cookie jar. The FBI even thought they might be able to arrest Siegel on charges of "Fraud Against the Government," especially since there was an ongoing investigation of bribery of a Civil Production Administration Official in Reno, Nevada with regards to the Flamingo's materials.

The FBI also heard that Bugsy was nearly broke and was looking for a $600,000 loan from a Utah company that had loaned the El Cortez $350,000. Del Webb Construction was on the hook for $435,000 and refused to continue building. The FBI, always listening, heard that the Nevada Projects Corporation was going into bankruptcy. The FBI was so happy!

Meanwhile, back at the ranch, Ben instructed Greenbaum,

"Listen, Gus, get $10,000 from Dave Berman and get $10,000 from the Golden Nugget. Then, take the remaining $45,000 from the Las Vegas Club race book and make out a check for $60,000 and another one for $40,000 to the Nevada Projects Corporation and date them November 1. Then, call Del Webb and tell him there's $100,000 ready to be cashed in November." Siegel was walking on thin ice in the desert, and he could hear it cracking.

At the meeting in San Francisco, Siegel and some friends discussed the issues and then got down to some serious poker playing, which went on until 4:15 in the morning. At the 10 am meeting, Siegel explained to the CPA directors that there weren't three buildings, it was just one big building, shaped like a big horseshoe (an ugly one at that), and they were using the original January plans that were approved. Amazingly, the CPA wasn't able to find their copy of the January plans. Sometimes things go missing in the night.

Of course, the plans were substituted three times in three months as Ben made change after change, but Del Webb swore the March 1946 plans were the original January 1946 plans, and what could the CPA prove now? Also, any lingering questions about bribery were straightened out by Senator McCarran, who said, "I have the greatest respect for the job the CPA is doing, and with all the construction going on it is understandable that an error or two might be made." The following afternoon, the CPA officer who had first approved the construction and then put in a stop-order approved it again. All was well if Ben could just find some more cash.

Unfortunately, the new horseshoe shape wasn't lucky for Siegel, and neither was his redheaded girlfriend. Virginia was on edge and fed-up with the sand, the wind, and the long hours. When she couldn't take anymore, she left for Los Angeles and took a second trip to Switzerland. She took more cash with her.

Things went from bad to worse when the construction began to wind down. Ben pushed the crews hard so he could have the club ready before New Year's Eve, but there was a problem. None of the hotel rooms were finished.

Phoenix contractor Del E Webb, who was chosen for the project by Gus Greenbaum (who happened to get a nice finder's fee of

$62,000), was waiting for payment one Friday afternoon in Siegel's room when Virginia came in and started throwing everything that wasn't nailed down at Bugsy. She showed good delivery, but her aim was poor. Still, she was sick of the desert. He was sick of her. She yelled and rushed at Bugsy, who simply grabbed her arm and forced it behind her back while she screamed and kicked him with her favorite $100 heels. Eventually, the room quieted, and she slunk out of the suite.

When she did, Siegel called someone downstairs and threatened to kill them if they let her back in the suite that afternoon. Then he remembered Del Webb was waiting in the wings. "Don't worry, we only kill our own, Del," Bugsy assured his contractor.

Ben had borrowed and spent almost $2 million dollars by this time and knew he had to get the Flamingo open. He wasn't skimming anything from the project; he was broke. Broke in his terms meant he was down to the final cash Meyer gave him, $300,000. On edge daily, his fights with Virginia were loud and public; his lifestyle was an embarrassment to his backers. He simply wasn't used to giving orders and waiting for them to be followed. He was used to people jumping when he spoke, or he smacked and whacked 'em, which he did when the building and the money pushed him to the limit.

One afternoon, Marie "The Body" McDonald, his backup emergency girlfriend who was staying in a bungalow at the Last Frontier as his guest, told Siegel, a little secret about another man. She had been up the street at the El Rancho casino when Sanford Adler, the Mob front man, took a particular liking to her. The 22-year old starlet had just finished filming *It's a Pleasure* and was enjoying Las Vegas, but Siegel wasn't about to share her. Her story got worse when she told Bugsy that Adler had gone so far as to tell her, "Stay away from the Flamingo, gangsters run it."

Siegel's eyes turned steel blue as he stalked off to the parking lot and climbed into his black Chrysler convertible coupe and sped up the street. Five minutes later he found Adler, and without so much as a nod in his direction, pulled his revolver from his waist and thumped it against the manager's head. Two more hits knocked him to his knees, and Bugsy leaned forward and whispered something in his ear. Adler never told anyone what was said.

Del Webb and his construction company were now close to bankruptcy too. His lawyers and the Nevada Project's lawyers agreed: Webb would forget about the $770,000 profit he was expecting, and keep construction going if he was paid for all materials and his actual current costs. To finish the construction, Gus Greenbaum got a $500,000 loan through Tony Accardo in Chicago at 4%. That put just over $3 million into the Flamingo, and it wasn't even open yet.

With the money from Chicago, Siegel went ahead with his plans to get the casino and restaurants open on December 26th, the hell with the rooms. People could stay at the El Rancho or the Last Frontier. Ben chartered a fleet of Constellations to fly his Hollywood guests to Vegas for the opening, but his luck was horrible as a winter storm lashed the west coast and grounded his planes, and his big plans.

The Flamingo Showroom opening featured Jimmy Durante, the Xavier Cugat Band, and Baby Rosemarie. Rosemarie was waiting in the wings for her first number when a handsome but tough-looking gentleman walked up to her. He handed her a stack of $100 bills and told her, "Go learn to play some craps, honey." Too frightened to refuse, she headed to the table where an ocean of chips and waving arms awaited. After ten minutes she went back in search of the gentleman in the fancy Italian suit. When she found him, she mumbled something and returned what was left of the cash he had given her.

The fellow turned out to be Ben Siegel, and he was more than a little surprised by her, but the money he gave her was indicative of his current problems. There was a lot of money going out and very little coming in.

A few brave souls made the trip to the Flamingo's opening by car, including friends George Raft and Jimmy Durante. The casino was full for the opening at 5:00 pm, but with no rooms, those from out of town had to stay elsewhere, at clubs like the Last Frontier and the El Rancho. Locals had been looking forward to seeing the final product offered by this huge casino project, and its huge ego boss, but everybody who showed up brought their good luck with them. George Raft managed to lose $65,000 across the green felt tables, but he was in the minority.

Over the next two weeks, the casino lost over $300,000. Ben was a playboy, not a businessman, and his expertise did not extend to building or running a casino. Not only were the players on a hot streak, but the dealers were helping themselves to handfuls of chips. Experienced dealers and inexperienced pit bosses do not make a good combination for management.

Ben shut down the casino two weeks later, totally broke, and called in another $500,000 from Detroit and Chicago. He was deep to the tune of $3.5 million to the Mob now, but his shareholders were already forgotten about. He had sold 250 percent of the property and had no intention of paying any of the Straight-Joes a dime.

To improve his income, Bugsy raised the cost of his weekly Trans America Wire service to $150. Bookies and casino owners in Las Vegas took the increase with ease, but bookies on the coast were unhappy and let Dragna know about the unreasonableness of the situation, especially since most were also paying $100 a week for the Continental Service. Chicago took notice.

In February, Siegel spent the rest of the borrowed cash to finish the hotel rooms, but before the reopening he was summoned to Havana, Cuba, to see Lucky Luciano. Bugsy was fit to be tied. A fellow like him, being told to report to Cuba, but he went because he had to. And, because he still needed more money. He met with Luciano, who told him the casino was a problem, and so was the wire service. "We expect to see our investment very soon, and you need to let Chicago have the wire."

Bugsy flipped, he yelled, but he was trapped, knowing his last source of additional income was withering away. "So, what's my end here, I lose all my income and have nothing to show for the work I've put in?"

"Of course not, Ben, you've got your share of the bookies, but not the wire fees, and you'll get something from Chicago, we're not there yet, but it's happening," Lansky told him. He also said, "Ben, you've got your clubs in Las Vegas, and you've got cash coming to clean up the Flamingo, but that's the end of it." Siegel left fuming, but still relieved he would get another chunk of cash, even if it weren't enough to finish building. What he didn't know, was that he wasn't the only person in town to meet the boss. In fact, he was just one of 17 others, including Meyer Lansky, Tony Accardo, Frank

Costello, and Albert Anastasia.

A new opening took place for the fabulous Flamingo casino on March 1, 1947, when the hotel rooms were finished, although construction was still not done and Del Webb was on a payment schedule. The casino continued to lose money. Las Vegas was still a cowboy town, and locals decided they weren't too keen on a place where you had to take off your cowboy hat. They didn't want to pay $8 for a steak dinner, and they didn't want to be told to "move along" if they were just watching the action instead of plunging away with their cash.

Luck finally turned at the Flamingo's tables, and the casino cleared a profit two months in a row, $170,000 for the previous one. While discussing the take, Moe Sedway told Ben he was going into politics because the people in town loved him. "You're what?" Ben screamed. "We don't run for office; we run the politicians!" He cursed a blue streak at his lieutenant, getting angrier each minute until he grabbed the little man's suit jacket and waltzed him across the floor and out the door of the club's offices. And, Siegel gave orders that Moe was to be permanently barred from the club.

Sedway was back in a week (and would indeed hold office in Las Vegas someday), but things hadn't settled down yet. Virginia Hill found Siegel chatting up a busty, young cigarette girl in the corner of the casino floor and rushed towards them. When she got within striking distance, she did, and then grabbed the girl by the arm and swung her away from Ben. Next, Virginia scratched viciously across the girl's face with her nails and pulled at her hair. Bugsy yanked the women apart, but then Hill started kicking them both.

"Sure, save her young face you gangster," Hill screamed, as the now animated casino owner pushed her towards a side door to the hotel grounds. "You're a murderer and a gangster," she cried, "you all are!"

When she pushed back at Siegel, he gave her a backhand across the face, bloodying her nose. "I'm through with you, I'm going to kill myself," she cried loudly. Siegel forced her to his penthouse, and the casino went back to business like it was an everyday occurrence. Perhaps it was.

In the morning, Bugsy took Virginia to Clark County General

Hospital and admitted her for a drug overdose. She was released the following afternoon. When she got back to the Flamingo, she went to their room, packed several bags and a trunk, and headed to the airport. From Las Vegas, she flew to Los Angeles and saw her brother, Charles Hill, who was staying at her home with his girlfriend, Jeri Mason. The following day she flew from coast to coast, and Joey Adonis picked her up at the airport in New York. They spent the night together, then in the morning, she met with Frank Costello, who bought her first-class plane tickets to Paris where she stayed until told she could return.

The very next day, June 13, 1947, Tony Accardo announced the Trans-America wire service was shutting down because he now owned the Continental Service. Both services, the Continental and the Trans America, had been in business since Tony Accardo's group caught the Continental Press race wire's owner, James Ragen, Sr. in an ambush that left him filled with buckshot and bleeding profusely in 1946.

Ragen was rushed to Michael Reese Hospital but died three weeks later. His death was a surprise to the doctors since he had undergone successful surgery and was doing well. Apparently, since the shotgun attack hadn't killed him, the Chicago Outfit moved to plan "B" – poison. His autopsy showed traces of mercury in his blood, which got there via the Coke's laced with poison that his friends were bringing him each day. Previously, Ragen made a signed statement to the State's attorney in which he alleged that Tony Accardo, Murray Humphreys, and Jake Guzik, attempted to muscle him out of 40 percent of the proceeds of the Continental Press. No charges were ever brought.

As for the Trans-America shutdown, Siegel was livid that the Continental was now a part of the Chicago Outfit's holdings and the West Coast profits were going to go directly to Mickey Cohen. He had been pushed out of his own deal. He was defunct.

Ben spent the afternoon of June 20th with Allen Smiley and his lawyer in Los Angeles. That evening, Allen Smiley, Jeri Mason, Charles Hill, and Siegel drove out to Jack's Café at Ocean Park. The restaurant was new and provided complimentary newspapers for their guests. Ben took one with him. They drove to the Linden Drive home where everyone stayed for the evening.

Jeri and Charles were upstairs; Ben sat reading the paper while Allen Smiley sat four feet away. It was Virginia Hill's home, but she was still in Paris after picking a fight with Siegel and heading to the friendly skies. Outside, with his rifle propped up on the lattice work surrounded by tall bushes, a shooter waited patiently. Ben snubbed out a cigarette and leaned back. Smiley sat quietly. Then, the glass window pane shattered, and nine rifle shots echoed about the room, the bullets finding soft flesh and hardwood. One pierced a painting; one shattered a marble statue of Bacchus. Another crushed the bridge of Siegel's nose, while another of the five that found their mark passed through Bugsy's right cheek and sent his eyeball skittering fifteen feet away. Allen Smiley was not hit. When the shooting started, he fell to the ground and hugged the floor. He didn't stand for two minutes, and he didn't call the police for another ten.

The shooter crouched and ran back to the car where Frankie Carbo sat waiting. Carbo ground the car into gear, and they moved smoothly up to touring speed and headed towards California Coast Highway 1. The .30-caliber Army carbine rifle was cut down with a hacksaw as they drove, and its pieces were tossed from the moving car. They stopped to refuel in Carmel, grabbed a bite at a greasy spoon, and continuing to San Francisco. Once in the City by the Bay, they holed up in a seedy apartment in South San Francisco.

The following morning, they boarded a plane for New York. In the city, they spent three days at 136-05 Sanford Avenue in Flushing. After a tip, they hit the streets running and split company. One headed to Florida, the other to North Shore Lake Tahoe on the California/Nevada border. The FBI raided the empty New York apartment hideout on June 25, 1947, and continued following their footprints for years.

When the shooting was over, and the hit confirmed, a phone rang in the El Cortez and was patched over to Dave Berman. He summoned Morris Rosen, and they met with Gus Greenbaum at the Flamingo casino less than 20 minutes later. Business continued as though nothing had happened.

In Los Angeles, bookies all over the coast rejoiced, knowing they didn't have to pay for two wire services anymore, and now this, Bugsy was dead too? Mickey Cohen reminded them quickly that he was still taking a cut of their income. As for Benjamin Siegel, his body sat for five days as the Los Angeles County Morgue, unclaimed. When the Coroner's Inquest was over, Dr. Maurice Siegel, Ben's brother, who was a rabbi, claimed the body, and services were held at the Groman Mortuary in Los Angeles. The service lasted five minutes and was attended by six mourners: Siegel's divorced wife Esther, his two children, Barbara and Millicent, his brother Maurice, and his sister, Bessy. At the time, the police still had not returned two strange, 14-carat gold keys with "BS" monogrammed at the top, which they found in Siegel's pocket. What they went to has never been disclosed.

Months later, Beverly Hills Police Chief Clinton H. Anderson said, "The gun used to kill Mr. Siegel, a 30-30 carbine, is an unusual type of firearm, though it is kept in all police arsenals." The FBI ran ballistics tests on several similar weapons but found no perfect matches. However, months after the shooting, Chief Anderson took a trip to New York and stated, "I know who did it, now I have to wrap up enough evidence to justify an indictment."

He further stated that his informants were convinced that he was slain on orders from The Committee, and that meant Charles Lucky Luciano. They further claimed that when Bugsy went to Cuba while the Flamingo was still being built and was seriously short of cash, he demanded that Luciano put up more money, and when Luciano declined, Siegel threatened to tell the papers what he knew about the Mob.

Anderson's statements prove that his informants were as bad as the FBI's, who continued to send agents to every government department investigating Siegel's death on wild goose chases from coast to coast. Every new wrinkle, every crook captured with any tie to Las Vegas or Siegel became a suspect, and newspaper reports were commonly used to do nothing but sell more papers. The truth was, that as usual money makes the world go round.

In April of 1947, as the club started working its way into the profit column, Luciano gave the approval for Meyer Lansky to send another $650,000 to Siegel to pay off the construction, but Ben was careful with the cash, knowing it was the last he would ever see. He stashed $300,000 with a friend, giving him specific orders to return it to Lansky if he wasn't able to do it himself. On May 6, 1947, Siegel's check from the Flamingo to Del Webb Construction for $100,000 bounced. On June 16, Ben wrote another check to Del Webb for $50,000, knowing it wouldn't clear the bank. His resort was bankrupt, and he too was close. He didn't have to fret too long. His day of reckoning was less than 100 hours away.

With Bugsy gone, Sanford Adler of the El Rancho took over as the front for the new bosses, along with Charles Resnick and James West. Together they bought-in for fifty percent of the Flamingo. Greenbaum and the lawyers explained the deal to the new owners. They had to put up 10 percent of the purchase price for their half of the business. Adler's end was $195,000 cash. The remaining 90 percent was a loan they were to make payments on. Together they owed nearly $2.5 million; the Mob held the other half. It was a nice deal, as long as they didn't mind someone else running the casino, and the count room.

Adler and his wife took up residence in Siegel's third-floor penthouse suite with the bullet-proof windows overlooking the pool, the steel-lined walls, the escape tunnel in the walk-in closet, and the floor-safe for any extra cash that needed a home.

From a spot in his room at the Last Frontier, "Fat Irish" Green, a sometime bodyguard and race book operator for Bugsy, took out the suitcase he was holding for Siegel. He boarded a plane for New York and met with Meyer Lansky in Frank Costello's office where the suitcase was opened. Inside sat $300,000 in cash. Lansky was so happy to see the money he called the El Cortez and told them to set Mr. Green up with Penthouse 1, for life. Oh, and free food for life too.

Lansky's word was good, and even after Jackie Gaughan purchased the property in 1963, Fat Irish Green (who was getting fatter and fatter) was allowed to stay in the hotel, gratis. Benny Binion offered to take the Fat Man in for meals, and Mr. Green ate at the Horseshoe for the rest of his life, for free. Of course, this wasn't uncommon. Even Moe Sedway admitted to the Kefauver Committee, "I get my room; I get my board." You're an owner; you don't pay for nothing!

Unfortunately for little Moey, the Kefauver Committee hearings were too much for him. He died shortly after trying to explain the race wire and how bookies paid for it. Moe said he paid, "$900 a week for him (Siegel) to sell me the exclusive rights to serve Las Vegas," but after Siegel was killed, he had to pay $2,500 a week just for the wire at the Golden Nugget, and then a month later "the guys" (Chicago) wanted double.

Mr. SEDWAY. We had no difficulty when he was alive.

Mr. HALLEY. You had no difficulty at all?

Mr. SEDWAY. No, sir.

SENATOR WILEY. Why were they afraid of Siegel?

Mr. SEDWAY. I don't know.

SENATOR WILEY. Who was afraid of Siegel?

Mr. SEDWAY. They wasn't afraid. They just got along. Whenever he made a deal, he kept his word, and they went along with him.

Most everybody went along with Bugsy. When you have a guy with a twenty-year history of killing people to get his way, it just makes sense to get along. It's the way the Mob-operated and prospered.

Back at the Flamingo, Adler thought he had control, but Greenbaum, Sedway, and Rosen ran the business, much to the chagrin of Sanford Adler. He hated that the pit bosses were in charge. Nobody argued with the pit boss. Not the dealers, not the restaurant manager, not the players. If the pit boss wanted to see a cocktail waitress in his office for a quickie, she went, or she didn't work – anywhere in Vegas.

Meanwhile, Adler hung on to his ownership like grim death, hoping he could somehow get control. One evening he pushed his way into the pit and got in Greenbaum's face about a high-roller's RFB comp (room, food, and beverage). Gus listened for thirty seconds, and when Adler didn't stop complaining, he punched him, right in the face, knocking him woozy and to the floor. Then Greenbaum said, "Throw this bum out," and that's just what two armed security guards did. He was still shouting as he was tossed out the door. Gus shouted in response, "You better get the hell out of Las Vegas, buddy, and never come back."

Adler steamed, he schemed, he fled to Los Angeles. Then he

drove to Carson City, Nevada to protest his dismissal to the new Tax Board in charge of gaming licenses. They asked him to put his request for a hearing in writing and to talk softly so he could be ignored. They were already bought and paid for. Adler's time in Southern Nevada was over. He scraped up his available cash, sold his home in Las Vegas, and moved to Reno, where he bought the Club Fortune at the corner of Second Avenue and North Virginia Street.

With Adler gone, Greenbaum got a better deal from his bosses. He took out a personal loan of $1 million and made a deal with Chicago that NY agreed to, including Lucky Luciano, Frank Costello, and Meyer Lansky, who had the final say-so on the Bugsy going-away party. The loan helped keep the Del Webb Corporation happy, as the club had been on a payment schedule that was overdue. It also paid for the construction of 115 new rooms, which greatly increased the club's ability to keep customers happily drunk and in the casino.

The next year the club showed a profit of $4 million, even after the New York and Chicago groups had gotten their skim. Las Vegas would boom over the next ten years as more properties joined the Flamingo on the "Strip."

In 1948, The Mob picked-up the Thunderbird Casino for a song (actually $160,000). The small club across from the El Rancho opened on Sept. 2, 1948. Guy McAfee, Tutor Scherer, Marion Hicks, and Clifford "Big Juice" Jones built the club on a shoestring, and it only took a single night for the shoestring to break. By 9:30 pm of the grand opening, they were well on their way to trouble as two competing casino owners, Jake Katleman and Farmer Paige, watched the dice on the craps table dance happily for two hours. When the table had received three "fills" of new chips, and those chips had made their way over to Katleman and Paige, they quit the game and hit the cage.

Their haul? More than $160,000 that the owners couldn't pay. The only person they knew who could handle the payoff was Meyer Lansky, whom they reached at his penthouse suite atop the Hotel Nacional in Havana. "Sure, I'll be your partner," Lansky said, "and make sure you get my brother Jake a good job." After that, Jake Lansky was listed as the "casino manager," and he fit the figurehead role to a tee. After the Sahara casino had opened, he held the same position, placed there by his brother to keep an eye on things.

That single phone call was one of the most expensive ever, as the Mob then exerted its control over the Thunderbird for two decades, skimming millions from the table game drops as well as lesser amounts from the slot drop.

6 ALONG CAME A COWBOY

When the nation saw Bugsy Siegel's bullet-ridden corpse on the cover of their morning newspapers, they may have coughed up their collective Shredded Wheat, but it didn't stop them from going to Las Vegas for vacation. In fact, it made Nevada dangerous and exciting. Bugsy did more dead than most casino owners ever did for Las Vegas tourism while they were alive.

Benny Binion (born November 20, 1904), took a different route to establishing himself in Las Vegas history. He came to Vegas as a gun-toting cowboy with a nasty reputation but went to the final roundup remembered as a kindly grandfather type who took bets of all sizes and started the World Series of Poker. Go figure.

Benny spent his youth in Texas playing fast and loose with every law and the statute of the Lone Star State, which meant he fit right in with the people of Las Vegas. As for the Mob, they weren't too keen on him. He was loud, uneducated, and made the newspaper too often.

In Dallas, his competitors had a difficult time holding on to their territories. Binion was the Top Dog, and many a bookie just up and committed suicide or had a gun accident when Benny was around. Binion was either lucky, a faster draw, or just plain guilty. In 1936, one of those competitors was Ben Frieden, but he was killed by Binion and Buddy Malone. It was ruled self-defense.

In 1940, Sam Murray was making headway into Benny's territory, so Benny and Ivy Miller met him at the bank, but he never made it to the lobby. Murray cashed out on the steps, bleeding to death after Miller blasted him at point blank range with six bullets. Murray made the mistake of giving his bodyguard, Herbert Noble, the day off, and that's when he was ambushed. The cases against Binion and Miller were dropped for insufficient evidence on the District Attorney's last day in office. Problems with Herbert Noble went on for years.

Noble set up his own gang with Ray Laudermilk and had his own policy wheel, which didn't sit well with Binion. A month later, Laudermilk was killed in his car. Benny's friends loved bombs. Noble bucked-up and started paying Benny the standard 25 percent, but he also wanted to expand. Benny said, "No, and your fee's gonna be 40 percent now," which infuriated Noble, who responded, "I'll never pay that, Cowboy."

A week later Noble's car was peppered with bullets, but he lived, and his boys killed one of Benny's shooters in the barrage of bullets. Word on the street was that Benny was offering $25,000 for Noble's head on a platter. Next, a car bomb killed one of Noble's gang members, and another bomb left Noble a widower when he loaned his wife his car for the day. Timing is everything. The attempts didn't stop, and Noble was again ambushed, shot, and lived to tell about it. By then the man had more holes in him than a kitchen sieve.

Binion's luck turned bad in Dallas when the Chicago Outfit backed his rival in the local Sheriff's race so they could control the gaming. Benny was forced out of town. He arrived in Las Vegas in

1947, angry, dragging his wife, five children, and a ton of cash. He bought a house, bought into a casino downtown, and tried to fit in.

Back in Dallas, Noble went a little crazy after the sixth attempt on his life, so did the media. The killings were big news, and the Mob's top bosses were less than happy that Binion was setting up a casino in what they considered "their" town. As for Noble, he decided the best way to kill Binion was to bomb him, from the cockpit of a plane he bought just for the job.

Before he could act on his plan, Noble got ambushed again in a barrage of gunfire at his ranch, but still, he refused to die. After surgery, he lay in his hospital bed trying to recuperate when a sniper outside took several more shots at him. Now the word on the street was that Noble was being called "The Cat," and the little kitty was worth $50,000 dead.

Benny had made plenty of money in Dallas, had a good bankroll, and wanted to raise the table limits at the Las Vegas Club where he was a partner, but he was voted down. He moved to a new casino fronting Glitter Gulch, and Governor Charles Russell said, "The license is predicated on Binion's sworn affidavit and proof that he is not engaged in gambling in any other state where gambling is illegal." Wow, Nevada was strict. Shootings, car bombings, and other nefarious activities notwithstanding, they just wanted to make sure he wasn't involved in any illegal gambling.

Nevada commissioners fell all over themselves to accommodate new businessmen with cash ready to be invested in the Silver State. When Binion opened the Westerner Gambling House and Saloon, he was quickly licensed, but his luck faded after Cliff Helms, one of his bodyguards, killed Johnny Beasley, who was trying to blackmail Binion, in the casino's restroom. It was all too much for the Mob's top boss, who got on the phone with his paid representatives in Washington, D.C. and got the ball rolling to silence the cowboy from Texas.

Benny moved on to the Eldorado Club and the Apache Hotel, which he opened as Binion's Horseshoe Club. He set his limits higher than his competition as soon as his gaming license was rubber stamped back into action. To get players in the door, he called his old friend Johnny Moss. At the time, Moss was one of the best poker players in the country. He traveled mostly the Southern United States, played all types of poker, and won considerable sums of money. While on this lengthy circuit, Johnny would occasionally play in Las Vegas, if the stakes were high enough.

Nick "The Greek" Dandalos was another friend of Benny's. He was known to play craps and faro for days on end, and he was also quite a poker player. After winning huge sums of money from the likes of Arnold Rothstein and "Titanic" Thompson, the Greek was looking for "The biggest game that this world could offer." Benny told him he just might have what he was looking for.

The Horseshoe Club at 128 E. Fremont Street in downtown Las Vegas became the scene of just such a game, which Benny positioned close to the front doors to attract interest. Eventually, the game was going 24-hours a day, and several "money" players joined in from time to time, but the main action was between Johnny and Nick. Nick was a well-educated, high-rolling gambler. Johnny, with a third-grade education, was a methodical killer of high-limit poker players' bankrolls.

The game went every day for five months, rain or shine, hot or cold, crowd or no crowd. Sometimes they played fifty hours straight. Howard Hughes is said to have dropped by and taken an occasional peak at the game, but he didn't gamble or play cards. Cards were dirty and carried germs. By that time he had scrambled his eggs pretty well in two spectacular plane crashes. He was still smart enough to buy several large parcels of land, though, two of them on the Strip. He let them sit idle for fifteen years. Howard was many things but never was he in a hurry to consummate a deal.

After several days of nonstop play, Johnny needed fifteen to twenty hours sleep to recuperate. When he got back down to the casino, Nick could be found at the craps table. "What are you going to do, sleep your life away?" he would chide Moss.

Other poker players won and lost, but most of the money on the table was passed between Johnny and Nick. With upwards of a half-million dollars on the table at all times, Johnny began to make a dent in Nick's vast holdings. Eventually, after Johnny had won several million dollars and nearly half-a-year had passed, Nick made his now famous statement: "Mr. Moss, I have to let you go."

Nick Dandalos had better luck when he played Faro Bank, and he enjoyed playing at Harrah's Club in Reno. At one stretch he is said to have played almost continuously for 90 hours. The casino was always happy with the action Nick helped attract. By the 1950s, after breaking the bankrolls of many players, the only high-limit action he could find was at casinos. Playing craps was undoubtedly his favorite game, but the house edge eventually wore him down to a frazzle. Near the end of his playing days, he was often found in Las Vegas playing the minimum instead of the maximum. When asked about this turn of events, Nick simply said, "Well, its action isn't it?"

Back at the Flamingo, it was business as usual. Plus, the caliber of their players was improving. Hundreds of players with money to burn were coming to the casino from back east, ready to spend their cash. If they didn't bring enough cash, credit got arranged. At a time when houses in small towns could be bought for $2,500 or less, the Flamingo had hundreds of players with $10,000 and higher credit lines. Business owners, bankers, lawyers, they all came to town to gamble, drink, and get laid. The legends they had heard were true. The casinos catered to their every need. Of course, you had to pay back your credit.

If you didn't pay, you'd hear from the credit manager. He usually sounded like he was smoking a cigar because he usually was. If you couldn't' pay, he'd let you know he was going to call your boss, or your wife, to let them know about "The broads you was seen with in the club. A guy borrows 10-large, he's gotta' pay. A course if youse can't pay up, I gotta' send out Rocco and Ralph to fix this here problem in person, and Rocco, he don't like to fly in no airplane, so he's gonna' be mad right off."

Players usually arranged for quick payment. When they didn't Rocco and Ralph-types made sure the player coughed up the bucks, or they got their heads smacked. The collectors were called leg-breakers for a reason.

The Flamingo was making enough money to keep everyone happy from New York to Miami to Chicago, and the El Cortez, Golden Nugget, and Las Vegas Club were still pumping out cash too, but like clockwork, the clubs changed hands, including Binion's Horseshoe.

Benny fought a long battle and spent most of his fortune trying to beat the government's lawyers, but in the end, he was sentenced to a five-year term at Leavenworth federal penitentiary for tax evasion, stemming from his gambling activities in Texas. All other charges from his time as Top Dog in Dallas were dropped, but Nevada was forced to pull his gaming license, permanently. In late 1953, Benny chose an old friend and fellow Southerner Joe W. Brown to buy the property.

Brown remodeled the club in 1954 and put up one of the most photographed displays ever, a giant gold horseshoe with 100 $10,000 gold certificate bills, encased in plastic. It was first unveiled Dec. 11, 1954. Binion was a solid citizen in Leavenworth and returned to Las Vegas in 1957. Brown sold his $1 million display in 1959. Binion built a new $1 million display in 1964 when the family finally had control of the casino again. It stayed on display until Becky Behnen (Binion) sold it in 2000.

Brown wasn't happy about selling the casino back to Benny, but the New Orleans gambler was a man of his word. It took a group of 20 investors to make the change, with Benny's son Jack Binion representing the family's 25 percent. Jack was licensed to run the club as president in 1963 at the age of 26. Benny was a consultant, who kept office in the club's restaurant and was rarely far from the gaming.

In later years, Benny was known for allowing a player to set their own table limit. His rule was "Your first bet is your limit." The property may have been smaller than some of the resorts on the Strip, but the action was higher.

One player even asked Benny if he could wager $1 million on a single bet. Benny said, "Sure if you've got the cash, I've got the action." A week later, Willie Bergstrom arrived with a suitcase filled with $100 bills. It wasn't a million, but it was lucky. Willie bet the whole $777,000 on the don't pass line of a crap game and won. Then Teddy Binion and two security guards walked him to his car with his winnings.

Bergstrom made several other trips to the Horseshoe, always winning smaller amounts until he felt comfortable betting the full million. On that occasion, Willie again bet the don't pass line, but this time the lucky shooter rolled a 6-1, for a front line winner "seven," and Willie headed to the bar.

The last loss was too much for Bergstrom, and a month later he took his pistol and ended his life.

7 WILBUR CLARK'S DESERT INN

Wilbur Clark, no longer fronting for the Mob at a single casino, started work on a new club with his brother, a block down from the Flamingo. With his ego intact, he named it Wilbur Clark's Desert Inn, and the plans included a hotel, golf course, and plenty of casino space.

According to Wilbur, a dapper, white-haired grandfather-type with a flashy smile and clothes to match, he managed to accumulate a bundle of cash working for Tony Cornero off the Santa Monica Pier on his gambling boat the **SS Rex.** Then, he moved to San Diego where he bought some bars before selling them and heading to Reno and then to Las Vegas where his good luck and business acumen allowed him to build the Desert Inn.

There's some truth to the story; he was in San Diego and Reno, and he did start building the Desert Inn casino in 1947 with his brother and two other investors. Their total bankroll for the project was $240,000 which they spent in three months flat. After that, the graded lot and patchwork concrete for the main building sat for two years in the hot desert sun before a savior came to Wilbur's aid.

That man was Moe Dalitz (born December 25, 1899), who was associated with the Mayfield Road Gang of Cleveland and the Purple Gang of Detroit. Over the years, Dalitz, like many mobsters, used prohibition to fatten his wallet by all types of liquor violations including bringing Canadian whiskey across the river into Detroit. The success of his speakeasies brought gambling, and when Prohibition was repealed, some of those joints turned to gaming as their main income. That was fine with Dalitz, who had several successful casinos by the 1930s, but he also turned a few unions on their heads in his time.

He and his family owned many laundry services, and their workers were part of the union, and while the unions were supposed to represent the workers, money talks. In 1949 when the Detroit Teamsters local demanded a five-day work week for their workers, a strike seemed imminent. Moe contacted Jimmy Hoffa, and for $25,000 the problem went away. It cost much more for Hoffa to go away, but that was many years later.

The FBI kept detailed records on Dalitz, who they characterized as the "head of the Mayfield Road Gang," dating back to 1938. Dalitz denied to agents that he was ever a part of the Purple Gang of Detroit, although he grew up with several of the gang's members. He also told the FBI that he left Detroit for Akron, Ohio where he engaged for approximately four years in the bootleg alcohol business before moving to Cleveland where he continued to sell bootleg whiskey. The FBI agreed with his statements, and noted that Dalitz, "Muscled his way into gambling, pinball, slot machine, and other rackets. His major competitor in the slot-machine racket in Cleveland, Nathan Weisenberg was ambushed and killed. Dalitz was never charged."

His contacts over the years were many, and he was accused of harboring Louis Buchalter and Jacob Shapiro while they were federal fugitives. Just a few of the gang's operations were race horse betting books in New York City, Saratoga Springs, New York, and Miami, Florida. They also owned casinos like the Thomas Club in Ohio, Frolics Club in Miami, and Merchants Café in Newport, Kentucky.

Dalitz met with Clark in Vegas, and then Clark flew to Cleveland and met his other new partners, Sam Tucker, Thomas J. McGinty, Morris Kleinman, and Samuel Miller. Together they arranged to have the Desert Inn finished in record time. It opened in 1950 and soon had a championship golf course. Dalitz shared with Lansky, Lansky with the other families. While other crime families had a great aversion to putting any substantial money into a new casino for fear of having the rug pulled out from under them, Dalitz found the climate and culture in Las Vegas quite appealing, so plunking down a couple of million dollars was more palatable to him.

Clark was the perfect host and the perfect ego for Las Vegas. He was a legend in his own mind and minted 3,500 $1 slot tokens with his likeness on them. He liked them so much he made key chains and lucky bucks with his picture, then chips. The property was spacious, with plenty of parking right in front of the casino. It became a favorite of locals for meetings, and there were plenty of deals that originated at the bar.

There were also plenty of Hollywood types in attendance on any given weekend in Las Vegas. With stars like Ronald Reagan playing at the Sahara, Sinatra playing at the Sands, Jimmy Durante, Rosemarie, Joe E. Brown, Bing Crosby, Bob Hope, and Zsa Zsa Gabor often seen hobnobbing around, Vegas was the place to be in the 1950s.

Ava Gardner was another Hollywood bombshell who liked to visit the Desert Inn, and not always with her husband, Frank Sinatra. She said afterward, "With him [Frank] it's impossible … it's like being with a woman." Then again, she described Howard Hughes, who she had a relationship with at the same time, as being, "Painfully shy, completely enigmatic and more eccentric than anyone [she] had ever met." What happens in Vegas, doesn't always stay in Vegas.

As Dalitz and the Desert Inn gained fame, their guest list included people like Crown Prince Bernhard of the Netherlands and even the Duke and Duchess of Windsor. And then along came the sporting group.

Moe Dalitz was a big golf fan, playing the resort's course every morning and taking lessons from the club's resident pro, Howard Capps, who is credited with the idea of pitting the winners of the previous year's PGA Tour events in a Tournament of Champions. It was Dalitz and Allard Roen who came up with the prize – the most on tour – of $10,000. When the first year's winner, Al Besselink, captured the tournament in 1953, he was presented with a wheelbarrow filled with 10,000 silver dollars. Dalitz suggested he make a sizable donation to charity, so he promptly donated half the money to the local Damon Runyan Memorial Fund for Cancer Research. "Honest, I wanted to," he said.

Gene Littler won the tournament the next three years, including a 13-stroke victory posted in a driving rain. And, the event became *the* place to be, as celebrities like Walter Winchell, Bob Hope, the Marx Brothers, and a host of female starlets were soon seen at the Desert Inn. To help increase interest, the celebrities held a Calcutta pool, drawing the names of entrants and pitching their money into the pool.

After Littler's victory, singer Frankie Laine, who had radio hits like "On the Sunny Side Of The Street," "I Believe," and "Moonlight Gambler," won the largest Calcutta, a $95,000 hit that was ten times the amount won by his golfer for winning the tournament!

Down in Cuba, Meyer Lansky finally convinced Fulgencio Batista to let him run the National casino. Pan Am's Intercontinental Hotels Corporation took over management of the hotel in 1955. Lansky took a wing of the grand entrance hall to refurbish, which also included a round bar, plus a restaurant, a showroom, and of course the luxurious casino with chandeliers, deep carpet, and a new job for his brother Jake.

New chips were made for his front man, Wilbur Clark, and again they featured the smiling man from Las Vegas, who managed to visit the club more than once while it was in operation. Wilbur Clark's

Casino International opened with Eartha Kitt in the dinner theater, and flights from Florida were packed with tourists. The casino was a huge success. Dalitz and Lansky scored most of the income, while Batista's wife helped collect her husband's ten-percent fee nightly.

Around the island, casinos were going up faster than in Las Vegas, and why not? The government was matching, dollar for dollar, all construction costs. George Raft, Bugsy's old pal, fronted for the Capri casino. Everyone was getting rich but the locals.

8 TV'S DISORGANIZED CRIME

In 1950, US Senator Estes Kefauver chaired a new committee called The United States Senate Special Committee to Investigate Crime in Interstate Commerce. What a mouthful. The title itself was longer than the testimony of most of the crime bosses they called. The idea was to investigate organized crime that crossed state borders, something that the FBI was well aware of, and while the committee never came close to proving there was a nationwide organization of criminals, it did provide some exciting TV for a country learning how this new form of entertainment was going to be used.

The Kefauver Committee first stated: "There is substantial and strongly convincing evidence that organized groups of criminals have been engaged in many parts of the Nation in illegal activities, utilizing the channels of interstate commerce, and often operating throughout many States." You think?

In all, 600 witnesses were called to testify in 14 cities, with big names like Joey Adonis, Meyer Lansky, and Tony Accardo, arriving and mostly refusing to answer any questions "on the grounds that it may incriminate me." Frank Costello agreed to testify and not plead the 5th Amendment, but only if his face wasn't shown on TV. Instead, the cameras focused on his little dancing hands for several days. In a show of control, The Kefauver Committee had him arrive each morning at 9:00 am and cool his heels in the hallway while they found other things to do until after 3:00 pm when they would call him to testify.

After days and days of answering questions about who he knew, when he knew them, where he knew them from, Costello, who they stated was the "King of Organized Crime in New York," was asked what he had done for his country. He said simply, "Paid my tax."

Eventually, Costello had heard enough questions, even if The Kefauver Committee hadn't heard enough answers. He said," I'm not going to answer any more questions. You say I'm not under arrest and I'm going to walk out," which he did. In August of 1952, he was convicted of contempt of Senate charges and received a sentence of 18 months in jail.

In Miami, The Kefauver Committee had better success with their 13 witnesses, and later stated:

"The group operating at the Colonial Inn, which has since transferred its activities to the Club Greenacres and the Club Boheme, included Frank Erickson, of New York; Joe Adonis, of New York; Meyer and Jake Lansky, of New York; and Mert Wertheimer, of Detroit. These operations show tremendous profits; the net reported income totaling $348.821.48 in 1948 and $509,073.44 in 1949. Also, they operated what was known as the "big New York craps game," conducted by William Bischoff and Joseph Massei. This cash operation of a single craps table yielded $222,056.47 in reported income for the 1949 season."

By comparison, Clifford "Big Juice" Jones, lieutenant governor of Nevada, stated that his 1 percent interest in the Golden Nugget in downtown Las Vegas made him $12,000 in 1949. This was learned during testimony in the City of Sin, where only six witnesses testified. Four in the first two hours before the members went traipsing off to see Boulder Dam, and two afterward. Then the Senators held a press conference, folded up their tent, and moved on. Vegas must be clean!

Later, The Kefauver Committee found Moe Dalitz. They had looked for him in Cleveland and Las Vegas, but he explained that he lived in Detroit, but had most recently been in Phoenix, Arizona.

THE CHAIRMAN: "Where did you stay when you were in Phoenix, Mr. Dalitz?"

Mr. DALITZ. At the Nevada Biltmore.

That was the only straight answer Dalitz gave. He bobbed and weaved, he questioned the questions, and he said that he and Mr. Tucker and Mr. Kleinman owned 39 percent of the Desert Inn. When questioned further, he added that Mr. McGinty and Mr. Jones owned 20 percent. That left Wilbur Clark with 41 percent. A healthy amount, but Clark never got more than 2 percent of what the resort made.

As for the cost of building, Dalitz stated that his group paid the construction costs in 1950 and that they spent a total of 1.2 million. If that's true, how did the Flamingo blow over $4 million? *Time* magazine estimated the cost of the Desert Inn's construction at $5 million. If that's true, it again points out that Siegel wasn't skimming any cash, only Virginia Hill was, and what she took probably wasn't much. Alright, maybe a few hundred thousand.

While somewhere between 20 and 30 million people caught portions of the Kefauver hearings in bars, taverns, storefront windows, and at home, nobody could have enjoyed seeing Frank Costello's dancing hands as much as seeing the flamboyant Virginia Hill in a big floppy hat and mink stole explaining that when she was with friends, like Ben, "They paid for everything, bought me a house in Florida, bought me things, gave me some money too."

SENATOR TOBEY: "And you know Joe Epstein, you said he gave you money, and he gave you money to bet horses. Do you still bet the horses?"

WITNESS: "No, I'm afraid I'll win and then they'll say I made more money than I did."

The crowd tittered at Miss Hill's response and a good time was had by one and all as the high-pitched voice laced with a Southern drawl echoed around the room. Her other comments were not met with laughter in the courthouse.

SENATOR TOBEY: "But why would Joe Epstein give you all that money, Miss Hill?"

WITNESS: "You really want to know?"

SENATOR TOBEY: "Yes, I really want to know."

WITNESS: "Then I'll tell you why. Because I'm the best cock sucker in town!"

There weren't too many laughs in the 11,000 pages of transcripts produced by The Kefauver Committee, but it was obvious that gambling, and crime, paid. It was obvious that there was some hierarchy of criminals and those gangs in different parts of the country were working together. Although the FBI had always denied there was a Mafia, it was apparent to every person who saw the hearings or read the newspapers or glanced at *Time* magazine (which put Kefauver's face on its cover), there was something big going on.

For the Mob, it was an embarrassment, and it was expensive, and while they didn't start shutting down their illegal casinos, local law enforcement eventually got around to that over the next ten years. In Nevada, the state finally started the Nevada Gaming Control Board to regulate gaming and licensing across the state.

9 WHERE'S THE FBI?

Anyone living in the 1940s and 1950s knew there were powerful groups of individuals who were organized for the advancement of criminal activities. It was obvious that those activities quite often skirted state lines. What we know now about the Mob, the FBI, and other government agencies knew 70 years ago, but they were never moved actually to take action.

Today, the FBI lists as its first three responsibilities some very interesting things. Under Title 18, United States Code, Section 659, is theft from interstate shipment. That means every time a gang hit the local airport to steal a shipment of goods as though it was their own personal ATM, the FBI should have been taking down the Mob, but they didn't.

The next area of responsibility is the fencing of those products, like cigarettes, razor blades, the things everyone needed and wanted to buy from the back of the stolen truck at half price. The Hobbs Act, interference with commerce by threats of violence, happened every day at truck stops, union meetings, and while hijacking those loads of radios and TV's that somehow disappeared each night, but the thieves rarely got caught. Even when those stolen goods went across state lines. So, what's up with that?

The Bureau Began in 1908

The Bureau of Investigation was created in 1908 by Attorney General Bonaparte, who appointed Stanley Finch as its first chief. They had good intentions, and the newly hired staff of fifty was given the task of stopping white slavery and prostitution through enforcement of the Mann Act, which prohibited interstate transport of females for "immoral purposes." Agent J. Edgar Hoover was appointed the Director in 1924 before the Bureau became the United States Bureau of Investigation, and then the Department of Investigation, and finally the Federal Bureau of Investigation, or FBI, in 1935.

Hoover was born January 1, 1895, in Washington, D.C., but his home life was less than happy. His mother was stern, domineering, and demanded that J. Edgar conforms and become "a great success, instead of a wallflower." Young Hoover often stuttered his words and took great offense to references about his father, who was mentally ill and clung, strongly to his morally righteous mother. Although J. Edgar obtained a law degree and then a Master of Laws degree from George Washington University Law School in 1917, he spent much of his time at home.

His mother, Annie, preached regularly to J. Edgar and his siblings about sin and sinners, and to appease her, he went to work for the Department of Justice. Edgar was inspired by the long campaigns against vice and pornography waged by Anthony Comstock, who at the height of his power was able to get the United States Postal Service to prohibit the mailing of anatomy books to medical students because they showed the human body in various stages of nudity. The horror!

Hoover occasionally sought the odd date with women, for the time being, seen with Lela Rogers, mother of actress Ginger Rogers, but it was all for show. Hoover clung to his mother, living with her until he was over 40. Strangely enough, the very sins and vices his mother had warned him about became his obsession. Author Truman Capote said Hoover was vicariously turned on by the smut he collected on others, and oh boy, did Hoover collect. On occasion, he wore his mother's dresses and left their home for a quick trip to town. Probably for undercover work.

Regardless of his predilections, Hoover carried great weight with Washington politicians, having made quite the name for himself with the FBI's War on Crime in the early 1930s. He regularly promoted his favorite agents, usually the brightest and best looking of the bunch, and placed his ultimate agent, Melvin Purvis, in the highest Chicago field office to find the Great Depression's most notorious gangsters, as long as they were working alone or in small groups.

Purvis corresponded regularly with Hoover, even when the Director put his arm around him or wrote what can only be described as sexual innuendoes to his favorite agent, whom he referred to as "the Clark Gable of the FBI." The FBI was both chastised and lauded in the press, but the bureau eventually got the job done with bank robbers and kidnappers. They hooked crooks "Pretty Boy" Floyd and John Dillinger, who were both shot in the back because the times allowed a "dead or alive" mentality. Others likes George "Machine Gun" Kelly, "Ma" Barker, and Alvis "Creepy" Karpis were also apprehended or killed. Bonnie and Clyde evaded the FBI but were ambushed by Texas and Louisiana officers.

Purvis and the FBI agents assigned to him were less successful at the Little Bohemia Lodge in Wisconsin when they tried to apprehend "Baby Face" Nelson. Not only did they open fire on and kill unsuspecting lodge guests with no connection to the gang, but Dillinger and Nelson both escaped into the night. One agent was shot dead after he drew his gun but didn't fire. The FBI found out later that his gun jammed and couldn't fire.

During his time with the FBI, Purvis captured more public enemies than any other agent in FBI history and was praised in the press, which infuriated Hoover, who may also have been spurned in the affection department. Hoover demoted him, so Purvis left the FBI to practice law.

Hoover moved his attention to a friendlier agent, Clyde Tolson, and the pair had dinner on J. Edgar's birthday (New Year's Eve) at the Stork Club in New York. Sherman Billingsly ran the club, with a large fee to Frank Costello, and was known to have his issues with privacy. Also at dinner, that evening was Walter Winchell, the radio and newspaper columnist who regularly trolled for gossip at the club, and he paid good money for the right information.

To that end, Billingsley had hidden microphones planted at some booths and even used two-way mirrors in the bathrooms to see the stars in action. He had refused dinner reservations to men who had been seen together through the two-way mirrors, but that wasn't the case with Tolson and Hoover. Instead, the sight of the two men holding hands made the likes of Costello and Meyer Lansky happy. Model Luisa Stuart saw Hoover holding hands with Tolson when they rode in a limo to the Cotton Club, and she passed the news to Walter Winchell.

Later, Winchell would become a favorite correspondent of Hoover's, who passed on little tidbits of information from time to time to the radio star. Winchell, for his part, kept his greatest story secret. Of course, Hoover by that time had his arsenal of information on Hollywood Stars, politicians, and business leaders, so he and the FBI were feared by many, but not the Mob.

Although Hoover had been using wiretapping since the mid-1920s to apprehend bootleggers, the FBI's cases were typically against mid-level hoods. The Communications Act of 1934 outlawed non-consensual phone tapping but allowed bugging. So, the FBI kept listening, and listening, and listening, but Frank Costello, Meyer Lansky, and Bugsy Siegel kept right on doing things their way.

Of course, the FBI was the very bureau to investigate the Mob's interstate activities, money laundering, and illegal casinos with profits going to other states, but Hoover and the FBI continued to deny that there was such a thing in the United States as organized crime, and he was against gambling. Still, Hoover liked to visit the Del Mar race track where he and Tolson mingled with good-looking movie stars like Bing Crosby and Gary Cooper, and he liked to bet the horses. He rarely read the tout sheets, but he won plenty of bets, allegedly fed the winners in fixed races by Meyer Lansky's operatives.

Lansky and Hoover's relationship was tenuous at best, but Lansky had nothing to fear from Hoover, due to his intimate knowledge of the Director's sexual persuasions. It is alleged that just about the time the Flamingo was stalled in the desert and Siegel couldn't get licensed; a photo taken through a wall-mounted fisheye lens was presented to Hoover that showed him, naked, in a compromising situation with Clyde Tolson. Although Hoover had left Lansky and Costello alone for years, the photo was enough to force the Director to help Siegel obtain his gaming license in Nevada.

When the Apalachin Summit was exposed (sorry, bad choice of words) in 1957, and dozens of high-ranking crime family bosses were arrested, Hoover could no longer deny the existence of the Mob. But some have questioned just what happened in that sleepy little upstate New York town.

Obviously, there was a meeting of the bosses, but strangely enough, Meyer Lansky wasn't there. Neither were "Lucky" Luciano or Frank Costello and if Luciano could get to Cuba, he could get into NY through Canada if he wanted. Both Luciano and Joseph "Doc" Stacher said later the meeting was sabotaged.

The heads of the families from Chicago, Detroit, New Orleans and San Francisco were also absent, places that had contracts with Frank Costello and his NY Family. No one connected gaming in Las Vegas to the meeting. The city was safe, and so was Meyer Lansky.

Hoover was quiet for years on organized crime, whether based on blackmail or the simple fact that his agents would have been susceptible to the bribes offered by a heavily-financed base of crime families, but after the Kefauver hearings in 1950 and 1951, the FBI created the Top Hoodlum Program in 1953. It didn't catch any top hoodlums. According to Hank Messick, a Lansky biographer, "In 1966, a young G-Man assigned to go through the motions of watching Meyer Lansky began to take his job seriously and develop good informants. He was abruptly transferred to a rural area in Georgia. His successor on the Lansky assignment was an older man who knew the score. When he retired a few years later, he accepted a job with a Bahamian gambling casino originally developed by Lansky."

Finally, in 1970, the passage of the RICO Act (Racketeer Influenced and Corrupt Organizations Act) took effect, and the FBI began investigating the crime families in major cities. Hoover died in 1972 before any major arrests were made or cases were taken to trial.

10 THE PRICE OF FAME

Las Vegas hardly took a hit from the Kefauver hearings. In fact, if anything, Nevada came out looking like the place to go, for both players, and mobsters that wanted to go legit. Of course, there were a few mobsters that still wanted to ply their trade, and a few even chose Las Vegas as the place to get rich, without gambling.

The first robbery of a Strip casino took place on May 28, 1951, a big day for two career minor-league thugs who decided to hit the race book at the Flamingo. Both men shared the same first name, Tony, and they both shared the same IQ, somewhere close to a dumb fish. Broncato and Trombino were from Kansas City and worked off-and-on for a small-time gang in L.A. Their plan was to case the joint and then rob it without ever being noticed, but they stuck out like sore thumbs.

After walking the property several times, Tony "B" and Tony "T" pulled their guns and forced their way into a small count room where they stuffed the morning's take, a measly $3500, into a duffle bag, and stumbled out of the casino.

After the robbery, they headed to Los Angeles without a care in the world. Broncato was quickly identified and made it to the FBI's Ten Most Wanted list on June 27, 1951, no doubt his greatest accomplishment in the world of crime. What's sad is that this bungling, inept robber could ever be considered a real threat. Still, the FBI apparently could only find nine crooks in the whole country worse than him. What were they doing with their time at the FBI?

Broncato turned himself in two days later, surrendering to federal agents in San Francisco. His lawyer posted $10,000 bond to secure his release, but Tony "B" was immediately rearrested on another warrant, and he went back to jail. A week later Broncato was out on a second bond, and he met with Trombino to discuss their very poor financial situation. Gus Greenbaum assigned a pair of men to tail the robbers. The Mob couldn't let thieves hit their casinos in Las Vegas, might give the wrong impression to the wrong element, and a message had to be sent.

Gus sent word to Jack Dragna in Los Angeles to "Snuff out the scum," and Dragna picked a no-nonsense killer for the job, Jimmy Frattiano. Jimmy, who became known as "The Weasel" after turning informant years later, got word to the Tony's that he was working on a bank job and maybe they could come over and pick him up and take him to a poker game in LA where they could discuss it.

When they arrived, Frattiano slid into the back seat of their car and chatted 'em up. Then he pulled out two .38 caliber automatics and blasted away, four shots in the back of the head each. Problem solved, the message sent.

Frattiano became known nationally years later when he turned into the biggest Mob informant the government of the United States ever had. He gave detailed information about all types of Mob activity, hierarchy, and rule. In the process, he admitted to being involved in over one-dozen Mob killings. Interesting fellow.

The Sahara and Sands hotels opened in 1952. The Sahara built on the site of the former Club Bingo. The Del Webb Corporation built the property at the cost of $5.5 million for Milton Prell, a jewelry-store owner, and supplier from Los Angeles. He billed the Sahara as the "Jewel in the Desert," and immediately got into a heated competition to sign Hollywood Stars to come and be seen in the desert.

The Sahara opened with Ray Bolger as their top act, and at the Sands, known as "A place in the sun," Jack Entratter was brought in from the east coast to be the entertainment director. He immediately signed Marlene Dietrich for $30,000 a week. It was an unbelievable salary and forced the other Vegas properties into a price war that still exists and forces us to pay $500 to see Elton John or Celine Dion play at Caesars. Thanks, Jack.

On the other hand, he helped usher in something else that was new to Las Vegas, but only because his huge budget at the Sahara forced everyone else in town to do anything they could think of to compete. At the Desert Inn, Harold Minsky (God Bless him) fought back by having his dancers bare their breasts in his showgirl revue, Minsky's Follies. Guests found the show, well, titillating. Other casino showrooms followed suit, and soon topless dancers were as much a thing of Las Vegas as blackjack was.

The Sahara had the largest freestanding neon sign in town at 100-feet until the Sands opened two weeks later. Milton Prell expanded the Sahara hotel by 200 rooms as the property exceeded all income expectations and Las Vegas began to grow into its own. Del Webb was so flush with cash from all the building over a 15-year period that the company eventually purchased the Sahara in 1961 with Prell running the property until 1964. By that time the Sahara in Lake Tahoe was also open.

In the midst of all the booming casino growth, there was booming in the desert just 60 miles northwest of Vegas, where the US Government was testing A-bombs. Believe it or not, the bomb blasts were visible from the downtown area, and postcards were made showing the mushroom clouds in the distance with hotels like the Fremont in the forefront.

Back at the Flamingo, things ran smoothly even with the added competition and Gus Greenbaum's escalating use of heroin. Just like in the movie *The Godfather*, he was banging cocktail servers two at a time, and the customers couldn't get a drink. Sometimes they couldn't get their coats back because the door to the coat check was barred shut. The coat check girls were always under pressure to please the bosses.

The Flamingo was doing great, but Tony Accardo was worried. Gus still owed him $900,000 and was now seen around town blowing cash like it was sand in the desert wind when he was *in* town. To try and keep his wife happy, Gus took longer vacations back home in Scottsdale, Arizona, where there were fewer girls and gambling, but more drugs. His wife arranged to have him picked up at a local bar, sometimes by a friend named William Nelson. He was a friend of Barry Goldwater's and enjoyed Gus's company. Most of his friends knew him as Willie Bioff, a former labor leader from Hollywood who extorted millions for the Chicago Outfit.

Unfortunately for the Chicago boys, Bioff was indicted in 1943 for tax evasion, extortion, and racketeering. Rather than taking the rap alone, he rolled over on his bosses, including Johnny Rosselli, Frank Nitti, and even Frank "The Waiter" Ricca. It was unfortunate for Greenbaum too.

Chicago boss Tony Accardo asked Gus to head the group at their new Riviera casino, on the Strip between the Desert Inn and the Flamingo. The Riv seemed to have the same problem the Flamingo did when it opened, money leaking everywhere. Gus declined, but Tony reminded him of the $900,000 he owned. Gus still declined. Nobody had ever told Mr. Accardo "no," twice.

The next week, Gus's brother, Charlie, found his wife dead, propped up on their bed. She had been killed. Message sent. Gus returned to Las Vegas, but he was steaming. With Joe Rosenberg and Dave Berman as new casino managers, quick changes came to the Riviera. No longer were the previous owners allowed to gamble in their own casino and then tear up their markers. Real high rollers were contacted and convinced to visit the new club with the incentive of free booze and broads. Even free airfare if that's what it took.

Most of the player names came from records Greenbaum took

from the Flamingo when he left. Player lists were as good as gold. Business was business, and Greenbaum was able to pull something like this on Thomas Hull who had purchased the Flamingo. He was not, however, able to get away with such tactics with his Chicago partners.

When Gus brought in Willie Bioff as the entertainment director, he ruffled a few feathers in Chicago. Marshall Caifano came to town and told Gus his latest move was, "Shit, plain and simple," but Gus didn't care; he was high most of the time.

On a strangely cold morning in November of 1955, Willie Bioff jumped into the cab of his pickup truck at his Phoenix home and turned the key. Bits and pieces of his body and the truck were found nearly a block away from the explosion. Again, the message sent.

Now Gus spent most of his time at the bar in the Riviera, and this time it was Johnny Roselli who came to visit. "Gus," he said, there's a gentleman's way out. "Sell your 27 percent and move on, everything will be forgiven," he said, "even the skimming."

"I can't this town is in my blood, Johnny," Gus said.

Roselli, always well-dressed and smooth as silk, used to hand out his business cards when asked about his profession. They had one word on them: Strategist.

Marshall Caifano, Johnny Roselli, and Tony Accardo had a sit-down. They discussed the issue with Lanksy, who said: "Go." Marshall Caifano went. A few days later a plane from Miami arrived in Phoenix. Two men got out and climbed into a car waiting for them in the private plane's hangar.

On December 3, 1958, Pearl Ray, the Greenbaum's housekeeper, arrived for work. The TV was blaring, but no other sound came from the house. She found Gus in the master bedroom, clad in his usual silk pajamas. He was stretched across two joined twin beds, pillows on either side of his head, holding it still. His neck was sliced completely through the muscle and tendons and down to his spinal cord.

Down the hall, Mrs. Ray found Bess Greenbaum, face down on a floral couch. Her hands were tied severely behind her back with one of Gus's silk ties. Her throat, too, was slashed open, but her skull had also been bludgeoned with a heavy bottle. The murder weapon, a knife from the kitchen, lay on a plastic bag. Surrounding her head were two pillows and a bathroom towel, which had kept the flow of blood from a beautiful oriental rug. It was apparently worth more than her life.

As the Mob's chief enforcer, Marshall Caifano took care of plenty of problems over the years. He was brutal, but he was patient. Mob hits don't happen on the spur of the moment. There has to be a sit-down, there has to be agreement. These things take time. As Caifano said more than once, "We forgive nothing."

Up in Reno, the Bar of Music on North Center Street in Reno sold for an amazing $150,000 after being open for just six months, but that was the usual smokescreen to make it appear more valuable to resell to someone else. Casinos in Lake Tahoe were sold like so many hot potatoes to launder dirty money, and to get "straight" investors who could front for Mob owners.

At South Shore, while a few casinos like the Stateline Country Club and Harvey's Wagon Wheel were around for years, smaller properties came and went, changed names, owners, tax rolls, and licensees on a dizzying basis. Just a few of the names in the 1940s and '50's were: Tahoe Plaza, South Tahoe Casino, Tony's, Dopey Normans, Main Entrance, Sky Harbor, Tahoe Village, Gateway Club, Twin States, Circus Room, Itahas, and Tahoe Stardust. The Tahoe Village had a revolving door of owners, and names, like the Casino de Paris'.

Under that name, Frank Sinatra started on his first comeback trail, but his voice was weak, and he got heckled from the small crowd. In his usual, classy style, he stormed off the stage mid-song and refused to return to Lake Tahoe. He kept his promise until buying into the Cal-Neva Lodge in the late 1950s.

In 1947, "Russian Louie" Strauss was denied a license to run the Tahoe Village, but that didn't stop him from making deals. He fronted for the boys back east, so things could be worked out. He had spent years working for Bugsy Siegel and Tony Cornero and brought in Harry Sherwood to get the license. Sherwood wasn't very well liked by Cornero after he staged a successful robbery of one of his floating casinos off Long Beach, California in 1936, but he was accepted. Besides, Sherwood had a marker-debt of nearly $80,000 at the Flamingo, and Greenbaum and Lansky were waiting for payment.

Eventually, they put pressure on Russian Louie to get Sherwood to make good on his marker while the Tahoe Village was doing well in July of the 1947 summer season. According to Russian Louie, the club's books didn't look right, and there were partners that wanted their cut. Someone was skimming, and only Sherwood and Russian Louie had access.

Near the end of the summer and the good income, Louie and Sherwood had a knock-down-shoot-'em-out fight. Sherwood did the knocking down. Louie did the shooting. One slug from Strauss's gun passed through Sherwood's right elbow and lodged next to his heart.

When questioned by the police, Strauss claimed he had confronted Sherwood about the $100,000 in investor's money that his partner had gambled away. He also claimed that the 250-pound Sherwood had knocked him down, and only then had he drawn his gun and fired two shots in self-defense.

Doctors removed the bullet from Sherwood's chest, but the operation left him paralyzed from the waist down. During surgery, Russian Louie left town. He was caught in his truck at the California border, towing a trailer, and in the company of his 18-year old girlfriend, a chorus girl Strauss claimed was his bookkeeper.

Sherwood never recovered, and Strauss went on trial for murder. A Nevada judge ruled, "No evidence was produced to show who fired the fatal shot." Louie walked out of court a free man. Afterward, Strauss returned to Las Vegas where he was often in the company of Marshall Caifano, who kept a close eye on him. They came up with a new front man for the Tahoe Village, but neither Caifano nor Meyer Lanksy was happy. They lost the $80,000 Sherwood owed the Flamingo partners, and a quiet investigation pointed to Russian Louie as the actual thief. Oh, and Sherwood was dead, but these things happen.

During a private poker game in Las Vegas, the deft-handed Strauss won over $75,000 and was happily heading to Palm Springs for a little vacation. Joining him in the black Cadillac limousine was Jack Dragna. Marshall Caifano was driving. The three pals wired ahead for three rooms before starting their trip. When the Cadillac arrived in Palm Springs, Dragna and Caifano only needed two rooms at the resort. Somewhere along the way, Russian Louie took a dirt nap.

Afterward, Meyer Lansky is said to have stated, "That's the last time a Jew will cheat a Sicilian in this town." Caifano took a vacation after that but spent most of his time in Las Vegas as the Mob enforcer for the Chicago Outfit, a position he earned by being a ruthless, sociopathic killer.

In 1941, Marshall found out that Nick Circella's girlfriend, a leggy cocktail girl at a bar in downtown Chicago, might be cooperating with the Feds on an extortion case. Her body was found later, tied to a chair, beaten, and then burned. Caifano had used a blowtorch on her. Russian Louie got off easy.

Editor's note:

(After the death of Frank "Bomp" Bompensiero in Pacific Beach (close range, silenced .22 caliber handgun while standing in a phone booth), Jimmy "The Weasel" Fratianno claimed that he and Bomp killed Russian Louie after he arrived in California from Vegas. That may be true. He also claimed it was at the request of Benny Binion, via Jack Dragna, because Strauss was blackmailing him. That doesn't make much sense since the last person that tried to blackmail Benny at his casino in Las Vegas wound up dead in the bathroom. Cost – zero.

Fratianno also claimed that Binion promised Dragna a 25-percent stake in a casino he was building in Las Vegas. Fratianno's claims made for good TV ratings, but they don't make much sense. There is ample evidence that someone offered $25K and then $50K to kill Benny's old nemesis Herbert "The Cat" Noble, and he was indeed killed by a bomb planted in his mailbox, and the killer was paid. If he was worth $50k, why would Strauss be worth the millions of dollars a 25-percent share of a new casino would be worth? Beyond that, the Chicago Outfit hated Binion, and Dragna in Los Angeles answered to Chicago. If they had a chance, they would have tried to hang the killing on Binion.

Final note – Benny spent most of his fortune trying to extradite himself from his legal problems and trying to avoid going to prison. He was sentenced in 1953, about the same time Russian Louie went away. It doesn't make sense that he would have had much interest in Strauss. It was common knowledge that he didn't have the money to open another casino, and he lost his gaming license permanently when he was convicted of tax fraud. Nice try Fratianno.

Marshall worked in Chicago with major hitters like Willie Bioff and Sam Giancana, and his own brother too, Leonard "Fat Lennie" Caifano. Lenny was a monster of a man who tipped the scales at over 300 pounds, and he didn't back down from anyone. How could he? The brothers got into the vending machine business and also bought hundreds of amusement machines like pinballs and jukeboxes with Giancana. It was a perfect business: hijack trucks loaded with candy, gum, and soda, and sell the product from vending machines at a good price, and then skim most of the cash off the top, why not, it's all profit!

In 1950, the Caifano brothers and Sam Giancana started moving into the Black wards of Chicago and taking down the number runners. Teddy Roe, a tough and respected loan shark and policy guy, stood up to the Caifano brothers. Eventually, they tried to make a deal with him, but Roe wouldn't budge, so the brothers hit his collectors, killing several. They also took shots at his wife and children, and when that didn't do the job, they bombed his house.

Eventually, all the beatings and killings came to a head, and Fat Lenny took a shot from Roe right in the center of the forehead. He died immediately. Roe went into hiding. In 1952, his doctor found that he had cancer, and Roe quit hiding. He saw his family, made peace with his partners, and took a stroll down South Michigan Avenue in a beautiful three-piece suit. Eight bullets turned his new suit to shreds. Chicago was a tough place to live and die.

As for Marshall Caifano, he was rewarded for his work with better jobs, and better pay. The FBI, still watching and guarding its secrets against other government agencies, knew about things in Chicago, and Special Agent Bill Roemer had a plan.

Caifano was a very well-paid, hired gun by the late 1950s, and he was in Las Vegas or otherwise indisposed on a regular basis. The Mob went through major changes in 1957, and the Chicago family saw Accardo step down to consigliere and Sam Giancana take his place as the head of the family. Maybe the power was too much for him because even though it was a major violation of the family's laws, Sam was interested in Marshall Caifano's wife, Darlene.

She was a big, raw-boned Kentucky hillbilly, but Giancana wanted her. Bill Roemer heard about their use of the Thunderbird hotel in suburban Rosemont as a love-shack, and he decided it would be fun to tell Caifano about the whole deal. Roemer had it in his mind that maybe Caifano would be so angry he would become an informant, but he misjudged Marshall, he thought he was human.

Instead of being angry, Caifano just smiled when Roemer told him. He took the whole episode as an honor, and a chance to blackmail his boss. Caifano wanted Las Vegas as his territory, and Giancana wanted him out of Chicago, so without ever admitting anything to each other, the two men got what they wanted. Accardo was truly unhappy about the selection of Caifano for Las Vegas. He wanted things handled quietly in Sin City, and Marshall was anything but quiet, but it came to pass.

Caifano changed his name to John Marshall and started buying expensive suits to saunter around the casinos in, but his taste was atrocious, he looked like a clown. He could be seen from a long distance with his bright green and yellow pants and heavy gold jewelry. He pushed his weight around the Mob's casinos and chased the front-men around their clubs when he didn't get his way. He grabbed showgirl's right out of chorus lines and dragged them to his room where he assaulted them. He kicked dealers when they lost too much, and he insulted Gaming Control Board members.

He had fights with several casino managers, connected and otherwise, and a running feud with Beldon Katleman, owner of the El Rancho Vegas is said to have ended abruptly on June 17, 1960. That night, while Harry James and Betty Grable were performing on stage, a suspicious fire broke out in a dressing room and the kitchen. It raged all night and destroyed the El Ranch Vegas.

When Chicago didn't do anything to slow him down, Nevada finally did. The Gaming Control Board had legislation passed that allowed them to bar certain "unsavory" characters from the state's casinos, and guess who the first character was? Bingo! Marshall Caifano, number one in the Black Book. Any association by licensees with people listed in the Black Book would result in fines and the possible revocation of gaming licenses. Nevada had finally acted. It was 1961.

Caifano refused to take the hint and continued to strut around the Mob's casinos. When he was asked to leave the Stardust one evening, he came back ten minutes later. The next time he was told to go, he went to dinner but still returned. This time, agents from the Gaming Control Board were on the property, and he was arrested, but the thick-headed mobster still couldn't get it through his skull that his days in Vegas were over.

To make matters worse, he did what his Chicago bosses never wanted any made guy to do, he hired a lawyer and sued the state over his arrest and his inclusion in the Black Book.

The added spotlight on the Mob was too much for Tony Accardo, who reassumed control over the Outfit and brought Caifano back to Chicago. Of course, the next enforcer in the city, Tony "The Ant" Spilotro wasn't any quieter.

Caifano lived out his remaining working days as a neighborhood bookmaker on Chicago's West Side and died in a Minnesota federal prison in 2003 at age 92.

11 LADY LUCK

There were plenty of happy times in Las Vegas, as the start of Carlton Adair's casino project, the Lady Luck. After two years of struggle, bulldozers were finally pushing dirt and sand around the hotel site. Adair thought the day would never come, but things looked better after he hired a tough, expensive lawyer from Reno, Mead Dixon, to help him get licensed to operate. Dixon met the partners, Stanley Burke, who owned the land, Frank Hoefus, the money man, and Warren "Doc" Bayley, who owned the Fresno and Bakersfield Hacienda Hotels and was slated to run the hotel. "Where's the capital?" Dixon asked.

Adair had designed the project so he and a few partners could run the casino, but the idea wouldn't fly without a real investment on his part. As a last-ditch effort, he tried to convince his partners that he did indeed have plenty of capital available, showing them a handful of diamonds he claimed were on loan from the widow of the Waterman Fountain Pen Company, to be used as collateral. Of course, if they were on loan, they couldn't be sold and were worthless as collateral, even if they weren't fakes. Adair was politely shown the door.

Pushed out of his own deal at the Hacienda, Adair did find some cash and a chance to front for the Mob over at the new Dunes. There, Major Riddle held 40-percent interest, and Chicago (and other families) took a fair share of the profits each week before any of the listed "owners" got a shot at it. Adair was surprised and disappointed when the Dune's casino license was almost revoked, but there wasn't enough evidence to prove his allegation that the graveyard crew kept losing a ton of cash to some guy from Boston. Adair was shown the door again.

Just as well. It was better to leave alive than face the wrath of one of the real owners of the Dunes, New England crime boss Ray Patriarca. The man from Providence, Rhode Island was tough, smart, and unrelenting. He was also unfazed by family ties. It is said that he ordered a hit on his own brother for not finding an electronic surveillance device placed by the FBI in his office. That's not someone you want to mess with.

Back at the building of the Lady Luck, things weren't getting any better. Frank Hoefus couldn't get a gaming license. That damn Gaming Control Board was starting to look at applications, and even with experience in gaming and a secret interest in the Golden Hotel in Reno, he couldn't get so much as a single vote for licensing.

Stanley Burke, the hamburger king from Sacramento, and Bayley, with his very successful hotels in California, managed to finance the project and the hotel opened in July of 1956, with Bayley taking over controlling interest. He renamed the Lady Luck the "Hacienda" like his California hotels, after convincing Roy Ritner, the owner of the Hacienda casino in North Las Vegas, to close his club and sell him the name.

The casino's next choice for a casino license was Jake Kozloff, but he had too many friends of questionable character. Jake had been at the Frontier and had "status" around Las Vegas, but he was unable to talk Bob Cahill of the Nevada Gaming Control Board into licensing him to run the new club. Finally, Mead Dixon hired someone with juice to represent Kozloff to the board. That person was Clark Guild, a snappy dresser, good speaker, and Governor Russell's brother-in-law. But Cahill still said no.

Even with Clark Guild representing him, Kozloff could not get licensed. It was left up to Kozloff to prove that he was qualified. "What did I do wrong? How can I get licensed?" he asked. To which the board replied, "Prove that you are qualified." After months and months, Kozloff gave up the fight to get licensed and in disgust, sold all of his Nevada holdings and joined Cliff Jones in two casino ventures in Aruba. Perhaps the Hacienda was lucky after all, as Kozloff and Jones lost their entire investment in Aruba in less than 18 months.

When the Hacienda did finally get licensed, it was a money pit, the quicksand of the desert forever swallowing up more and more investment capital. By then the Strip was built up to the point that *Life Magazine* devoted four pages to the death knell of the resort town (Las Vegas). What was the Hacienda to do? Hire the mob to run it? Not just yet.

Bayley stocked every gas station in a 200-mile radius with coupons and brochures about the Hacienda. He plastered pictures on billboards; he bought player lists, and he dispatched beautiful cocktail waitresses to show their skin and hand out flyers in nearby California towns. Then he tried making the Hacienda a family resort with 27-year old Dick Taylor as the resident manager.

He built a par-3 golf course that could be played at night under towering lights and included a $5,000 hole-in-one jackpot on a special 19th hole. Next to come were a miniature racecourse and the largest hotel pool in Nevada, a whopping 300,000 gallons. Nothing worked. The resort was drowning in red ink. Maybe they should have stayed with the name Lady Luck.

From the time the Hacienda started its long drive to get licensed until it was fully open, three more casinos opened on the Strip. The Royal Nevada Hotel opened by Sid Wyman was the smallest and struggled for three years before biting the dust, or being bit by the Stardust.

Up the street at the Riviera, the opening act for the April 21, 1955, Grand Opening was a man made for Las Vegas, Liberace. His pay was $50,000 per week. Even Orson Wells brought his magic and illusion show to the stage in 1956, but it took Gus Greenbaum and Ben Goffstein to turn a profit at the Riviera.

The Dunes came next, with a 30-foot tall Sultan standing cross-armed atop the front entrance. The group that financed the hotel stayed on, and the first real license was the same group of Sands partners. With Jack Entratter as entertainment director, the club presented Maurice Chevalier and Cab Calloway to guests in the showroom and Sophie Tucker, and Lionel Hampton followed. Rooms were $9. The dinner show was $6.50 and included one drink. A couple of bucks to the Maître d' got you a decent table; $5 put you up front. By then the property looked promising enough to entice Major Riddle to invest and front for Chicago in May of 1956.

Frank Sinatra knew Stanley Burke and wanted a piece of the Hacienda, but Chicago told him to say out, they would share some of the Dunes with him. He waited.

Beldon Katleman at the Last Frontier had the Gabor sisters playing in the showroom for the summer to compete with the Sands and the Sahara, and Las Vegas became an internationally-known entertainment capital. As such a capital, there was no better place to advertise than in Los Angeles. For the opening of the Red Skelton show at the Sahara, along with Anna Maria Alberghetti, Stan Irwin dreamed up a live billboard for the Sahara on the Sunset Strip. He built a miniature replica of the hotel's "Garden of Allah" swimming pool, and for months, young ladies were seen swimming and frolicking about in the mid-day sunshine of Los Angeles.

Meyer Lansky was so happy with the success of the Riviera casino in Las Vegas that he used the same name for his new 440-room hotel in Havana in 1957. Wilbur Clark was again his front-man; Meyer was listed as the Kitchen Director. He was listed nowhere else in the financial papers, and neither were his partners, Accardo or Dalitz.

When the $8 million-dollar project opened in late 1957, the 21-story hotel was the finest Mob-owned casino in the world. There were beautiful chandeliers and crystal across the ceilings, gold-leaf walls, beautiful Caribbean tile throughout, and the property had its bakery. Stars like William Holden and Ava Gardner flew in to see a new beauty, and Steve Allen even taped an episode of his Sunday night TV show. What's not to like?

Ginger Rogers headed the Copa Room Cabaret floorshow, and while the casino was busy and lucky, Lansky remarked later, "That Rogers girl can sure wiggle her ass, but she can't sing a goddam note." As it turned out, that was the least of Lansky's troubles, as 1957 was a pivotal year for Las Vegas and the Mob.

Too many casinos were opened in the mid-'50s, and there simply wasn't enough business to sustain them all, and still more were planned, but not on Mob money of course! Ben Jaffe, an executive of the Fontainebleau Miami Beach, bought one of the parcels along the Las Vegas Strip and low and behold he started building a casino. Before he could finish construction, he was forced to sell his share of the Fontainebleau *and* give up control of the new casino, but the resort opened in April of '57.

On May 2, Frank Costello was walking through the lobby of his Manhattan apartment building when he heard, "This is for you Frank." When he turned, a gun blast knocked him to the hard tile floor where he bled profusely from a scalp wound. The shooter, Vincent "Chin" Gigante, exited the building triumphantly but had given Costello just the warning he needed to keep from having his brains blown out.

Gigante was picked-up by police based on a passerby's description, but Costello refused to identify him as the shooter, and he was released from custody. Vito Genovese, who had controlled the hit, knew Albert Anastasia was furious over the assassination attempt and would seek revenge. He fortified his squad of goons and laid low. In Mob parlance, they went to the mattresses.

By then, the police were puzzling over a folded sheet of paper they found in Costello's pocket while he lay unconscious. The note said, "Gross casino wins as of 4/27/57 - $651,284," with individual wins for each gaming department. To be even more specific, the final line said, "Mike $150 a week, totaling $600; Jake $100 a week, totaling $400; L. - $30,000; H. - $9,000. The initial "L" stood for Meyer Lansky, the Mob's main financial wizard, and "H" stood for Murray Humphreys, Chicago's chief financial manager.

Costello was questioned about the note but feigned ignorance. He was taken before a judge but refused to offer an explanation. The judge slapped a 30-day sentence on the Mob boss for contempt of court. After some digging, the New York Police found the numbers matched the new Tropicana casino's gross win for the month of April, through the 27th.

In October of 1957, Albert Anastasia went for a shave at the Park Sheraton barbershop, and what a shave he got! With his face draped by a hot towel, two shooters entered the barbershop, and Anastasia exited the world. His photo on the front page of dozens of newspapers reminded readers of a picture from a decade earlier of Bugsy Siegel. Not too much had changed in those ten years. After Frank Costello had recovered from the assassination attempt, he and Vito Genovese made the peace.

The following month, the country became familiar with the town of Apalachin, New York; when dozens of men in expensive suits went running off through the woods trying to escape from a raid on their meeting of The Committee. On a lucky break, state troopers stumbled on a gathering of some very powerful men. Carlo Gambino, Vito Genovese, and Joseph Profaci were among the best known. Santo Trafficante, Jr. was also present, and so were at least 100 others. The local police and state troopers rounded-up 58, while dozens of others escaped through the woods with nothing more than torn suits.

The huge meeting of dozens of crime family members forced the FBI to finally admit there really was an overall power behind the Mob or Mafia, and that the heads of the families did meet, make decisions, and work as a group. Twenty of the apprehended bosses got fined $10,000 each, and several received prison sentences for "Conspiring to obstruct justice by lying about the nature of the underworld meeting." Yeah, that sounds strange. The sentences were all overturned on appeal.

Things continued to go wrong for the Mob at the end of the 1950s. In Havana, before Meyer Lansky's $8 million Riviera casino property had earned back even half of its cost, Fulgencio Batista lost his grip on the Republic of Cuba. Fidel Castro took over, renounced the casinos, then retracted his statement and said they could stay. By then the slot machines, gaming tables and even the parking meters in the city had been destroyed by happy vandals. Soon after that, Castro reversed himself again, refusing to let the casinos stay open.

In late 1960, the Republic of Cuba confiscated Meyer Lansky's (and everybody else's) holdings in Cuba. It would be up to his investments in Nevada to support him for the next twenty years.

Finally, in Las Vegas, the Hacienda property managed to turn a small profit by flying their players into town and stranding them at the strange configuration of buildings that made up a family vacation resort with a money-losing casino. Bayley, still buoyed by his other businesses, financed an air fleet of four Constellations, a DC-4, and two DC-3's to make regular flights from major California cities with the help of Henry Price, a struggling charter flight operator.

During the year of 1961, McCarran Airport registered 140,000 passengers through its facilities from the Hacienda airlift. The meager success of the Hacienda infuriated the other casinos, and soon the FAA was investigating if the Las Vegas Hacienda was engaged as an air carrier. The United States V. the Las Vegas Hacienda became a key case in FAA secondary air transportation regulation. The flights continued, and successful operations did too, now that the Chicago boys were running the casino.

As 1962 rolled around in Las Vegas, Lucky Luciano's last efforts to control his underlings from Italy ended when he died of a heart attack on January 26, 1962, at Naples International Airport. He had agreed to allow American movie producer Martin Gosch do a film biography about his life. Gosch never proceeded with the project.

Vegas and the Mob

12 TONY CORNERO

The 13th Hotel to open on the Las Vegas Strip was the Stardust. A lucky number for the Mob, since the casino stayed in their hands and produced more "free" money than any other casino ever did. And to think that the man behind it, Tony Cornero, was gone before the doors ever opened! But somehow his story is just right for Las Vegas.

Cornero was born in Lequio Tanaro, a small village in Northern Italy, but the family felt compelled to immigrate to the United States after his father lost the mortgage to their farm and home in a poker game. Oops.

After first being arrested at 16 for robbery, Cornero spent a dozen years in and out of jail, but the easy money of prohibition was too much to resist. He ran moonshine, bootleg, and saved every dollar until he could buy a boat. Pretty soon he was smuggling Canadian whiskey into Southern California with a fleet of freighters like the **SS**

Lily, which could transport up to 4,000 cases of bootleg liquor in a single trip. The liquor was unloaded past the three-mile limit into his speedboats, which sped the liquor to Southern California beaches. By the age of 25, he was a millionaire.

In 1926, Cornero was arrested while returning from Guaymas, Mexico, with 1,000 cases of rum in the hold of his freighter. After being sentenced, he told reporters, "I only purchased the illegal cargo to keep 120 million people from being poisoned to death by bad gin."

Instead of spending the next two years in jail, he escaped from his guards (for $2,200) and jumped off the train heading to prison. Then, he boarded a ship to Vancouver, British Columbia where he lived quite well among old friends for three years.

In 1929, on the advice of friend Cal Custer and his lawyer, John Harrah (soon to have a large casino named after his son in Reno), he brokered a deal with the authorities in California and did a two-year stretch in relative comfort.

Afterward, with Prohibition coming to an end, Cornero moved towards gambling. He and his brothers Louis and Frank moved to Las Vegas, Nevada, and bought some land and constructed a small casino called "The Meadows." Business was good, and the brothers invested in two other casinos.

However, the New York Mob families were already taking an interest in Las Vegas and wanted the Cornero's to share their good fortune. When Lucky Luciano and Meyer Lansky couldn't make a deal with the brothers, Frank Costello sent a messenger with a final offer. It was refused, and a day later The Meadows was torched.

Tony escaped with his life back to Los Angeles and decided to stay out of Vegas. Within a few months, he and three partners outfitted the first of their offshore gambling ships, the **SS Tango**, for entertainment and income. Anchored just over three miles off the coast of Long Beach, California, small speed boats brought players out to the slot machines and table games the ship offered.

Cornero preferred to be a one-man show and having partners was not something he enjoyed. Over a five-year period, the Tango provided a solid income for partners Bill Blazer, Cal Custer and Jim

Lloyd. Tony longed to own the Tango outright and tried to work out a deal to buy his partner's interest in the ship. Over a three-month period, several purchase options were discussed. None satisfied each man. Finally, the partners wound up in a daylong poker game for the **SS Tango**.

Tony was the first partner to bust out, and Cal Custer soon followed. The two remaining partners, Bill Blazer and Jim Lloyd, wound up as the dual owners of the **SS Tango**. Tony was less than devastated by his loss. He had made quite a fortune during Prohibition, and there was money left to start over.

He purchased a four-masted British ship, the Kenilworth, to re-enter the floating casino fleet and renamed the former fishing barge the **SS Rex**. Investing over a half-million dollars, the Rex was to become the favorite anchored nightclub in Hollywood. Advertised as "Just ten minutes from Hollywood," thousands of customers were carried out to the waterborne casino each night. Water taxis left the Santa Monica pier every five minutes.

California Attorney General, Earl Warren, became a thorn in Cornero's side when he called the gambling ships off the coast "The greatest nuisance operating in the country." Maybe he didn't know anything about Cleveland, Toledo, Detroit, Covington, Louisville, Miami, or Hot Springs, Arkansas. Regardless of those other illegal hot-spots, the US Coast Guard seized the **SS Rex** in 1939. Cornero should have realized the folly of operating on the waters, but in 1946 he again tried to open a floating casino.

The **SS Lux** was launched in 1946, but just two days after opening, Tony was arrested, and the 800 players on board were stranded. They continued to gamble. Finally, limited water taxi service was resumed to allow those on board a safe return to shore. Although Tony continued a court fight, the Coast Guard seized the **SS Lux**. Tony was out of business again.

He made plans to open a new illegal casino in Los Angeles, but Mickey Cohen wanted a meeting. After spending nearly $12,000 renovating a building, Tony met with Cohen. When they didn't see eye to eye, Cohen pulled a snub-nosed .38 revolver and placed it not-so-gently in Tony's left ear. They agreed that Tony would never open a club in Los Angeles.

With his options dwindling, Cornero called Orlando Silvagni, who owned the Apache Hotel in downtown Las Vegas. They agreed on a lease, and the SS Rex gaming hall moved towards licensing. The casino was voted down, but it was close, so Cornero bought the final vote he needed and opened his new club. Other club owners (read: the Mob) weren't too happy about Cornero in their midst and arranged a new vote. Strangely enough, the license was denied, and Tony was told to get out of town, which he did.

He moved back to Beverly Hills, California, severely short on cash. What he wasn't short on was chutzpah, and he found several people ready to invest in a new casino in Baja, but the local Mexican businessmen were no happier to see him than the Vegas Mob was. On February 9, 1948, Cornero opened his door in Beverly Hills and was handed a package. Once his hands were full, the two men at his door pulled their weapons and fired four bullets into his stomach. Somehow the feisty and unpopular man lived. He laid low for several years until the lure of Las Vegas was too much for him.

The town was booming in 1954, and he wanted to be part of the boom. He and partner James Bradley began selling stock in "Stardust, Inc." and started construction of a new hotel and casino. Tony applied for a gaming license.

His application brought immediate opposition from the governor and the Nevada Tax Commission. Also, the Federal Securities and Exchange Commission had questions about the stock the partners had sold.

At this point, as Cornero wondered how he would finance the rest of his hotel and casino, Meyer Lansky and Moe Dalitz laughed at how nothing had changed in the nearly ten years since Bugsy Siegel was floundering in red ink at the Flamingo. Now the two men watched and waited for Cornero to get desperate. It didn't take long.

Soon enough, Tony "convinced" Dalitz to loan him $1.25 million to finish construction, but he was still short of cash for the opening of the club. His new partners were happy to take a piece of the baking pie, but there was a new problem. The Nevada Tax Commission, which handled licenses at the time, turned Cornero down. To add a punctuation mark, Governor Charles Russell said, "As long as I'm Governor, Cornero will never get a license."

Russell, a long-shot to be elected, swept into office after a series of articles by Ed Reid about mobsters and corruption in Las Vegas, ran in Hank Greenspun's Las Vegas Sun. One of those caught on tape was Lieutenant Governor Cliff Jones, telling a prospective buyer of the Thunderbird Casino some interesting things. Jones asked the buyer if he had a record, and the man said, "A little narcotics, bootlegging, murder, manslaughter." Jones replied, "You're all right, but not until after the first of the year when Pittman takes office. Believe me; I've been called a lot of names…one thing nobody ever called me and that's stupid." Really.

Lou Weiner, Jones's lawyer (and previously Bugsy Siegel's), admitted even more on tape:

WEINER: "It's important to us to have Cliff in there because there are a lot of things that Cliff can get."

BUYER: "I know that on the back, Jake Lansky, Meyer Lansky, everybody's in it, on the Algiers, everything runs smooth. The Rancho over here, I got a good friend from New Orleans over there."

WEINER: "But nobody bothers them, they don't care. What everybody else does is their business."

WEINER: "Cliff can take care of it (Carson City licensing), but not…." (Until the first of the year).

WEINER: "They know Doc Stacher is in the Sands. What do you think; they don't know Doc's in there? You think they don't know Meyer and Jake are in the Thunderbird, huh?"

After the six-week sting operation, Reid started a series of twelve articles revealing the many conversations with "business owners" in Las Vegas. Pittman, who was destined to win the Governorship, lost to upstart Russell. Lieutenant Governor Clifford A. Jones tendered his resignation as Democratic National Committeeman, and lawyer Louis Weiner shook off the expose' and continued practicing law.

As for Carson City, the politicians set up the Nevada Gaming Control Board to oversee all gaming applications and appointed a former FBI agent to be the first director. It helped a little.

When Tony Cornero heard the Governor's response to his

application for a gaming license he replied, "I'll get a license or be carried out feet first." His partners chuckled among themselves, probably thinking, "Your proposal is acceptable."

While construction continued, Tony spent his nights shooting craps at the Desert Inn, sometimes happy, sometimes sad, and always loud and demanding. Moe didn't care much for the demanding part. During the game one night, Tony carried on a protracted argument with Moe Dalitz, who seemed to be taking the brunt of the abuse, but didn't look overly concerned. After a seven-out, Tony got back in Dalitz's face, took a big guzzle of his seven-and-seven, and then stopped in mid-sentence. He grabbed for the craps table rail, twitched his head back and forth, and collapsed to the dirty rug, littered with cigarette butts.

There were no attempts to revive the dying man. Cornero's doctor was called, and he asked that the body not be sent to the coroner's office. He was certain it would be Tony's last wish to be taken, quickly, to his family in Beverly Hills. He was. Again, quickly was the operative word.

The story continues that the cocktail server who witnessed the death and had brought the poor man his last drink, was quite shook up. To help her get over her grief, the casino sent her on a week-long stay in Cuba, where she had full rein of the facilities at Wilbur Clark's Casino National. Dalitz and Lansky got controlling interest in the Stardust Hotel and Casino, and poor Tony got a quick trip to Los Angeles and a fast burial. There was no autopsy performed to see what was in that last drink.

It was three years before the 1,000-room hotel emerged from Federal Bankruptcy Court and opened to the public on July 2, 1958. The process was drawn-out by the real owners, who couldn't drop more cash into the project with Cornero gone and the court system involved. Along came John "Jake the Barber" Factor and his beautiful wife Rella, of the Max Factor family, and they paid off the outstanding construction costs. The smaller investors, rumored to be in the neighborhood of three thousand, were quietly ignored.

Jake the Barber had a rap sheet longer than Tony Cornero's, including the time he orchestrated his own kidnapping to take down Roger Touhy, a competing gang head, and the time he was sentenced to 10 years in prison for selling $1 million in non-existent whiskey. He too, was denied a gaming license for the Stardust, and while it wasn't a big surprise, it was still inconvenient, but nothing that couldn't be worked out. When the Stardust did open, Dalitz held 22 percent of the Stardust Casino operation, which was operated on a lease basis from John and Rella Factor, who were running the hotel.

In reality, Tony Accardo, the boss from Chicago, fronted some cash of his own, about $3 million. Then the Stardust group changed names, and the United Hotel Corporation, the Dalitz group that owned the Riviera and Desert Inn (in the eyes of the Gaming Control Board), was licensed to run the property and the D.I. Operating Company was licensed to run the casino. If you aren't confused by that, you should be.

The D.I. Operating Company listed 13 applicants who put up the casino "cage cash" of $300,000. The names were familiar: Wilbur Clark (just 5.5 percent), Thomas McGinty, Morris Kleinman, Moe Dalitz, Sam Tucker, Allard Roen, Bernard Rothkopf, Robert Kay, Ruby Kolod, Clifford Jones, Joseph Bock, John Drew, and Milton Jaffe. Most were long-time members of the Purple Gang. Most had a piece of the Desert Inn.

Not on the list was one of Dalitz's most trusted partners in Cleveland, Samuel "Game Boy" Miller. He helped keep the clubs in Ohio going when Dalitz moved permanently to Las Vegas. Game Boy also purchased a house in Miami where he kept regular company with Meyer Lansky. In 1955, Game Boy tried to get licensed at the Riviera but was turned down. He turned his interest instead to the Royal Nevada where he took a silent role. The club struggled but still provided an untaxed profit.

Nevada regulators turned a blind eye to the final deals being made at the Stardust. They had an image to uphold as a safe and prosperous gaming capital, and a 1,000+ room hotel and casino to get open. The next month the Desert Inn purchased the Royal Nevada Hotel adjacent to the Stardust and diagonally across the street from the Desert Inn. The Royal Nevada was used as a convention center and also had rooms, slightly different than those at the Stardust. In modern terms, most of the rooms were nothing more than an inexpensive, motor lodge-style setup. Inside the Stardust, the casino was a good size, with room for 60 gaming tables, a keno lounge, a poker room, race book, and a restaurant.

The property also had a nice showroom with two additional restaurants, one a steak house and one a 24-hour café. Also, when the casino first opened there was also room for a bingo parlor, which drew a great deal of business over the first ten years the resort was open.

The property also had a large pool, obviously a big hit during the summer months when Vegas temperatures are usually in the 100's. When the show got out at 10 pm, parents often had to retrieve their children from the pool area (where the kids could order enough 25-cent hot dogs and hamburgers to make themselves sick) because the temperature was still 90 degrees at night.

All in all, the Stardust provided a friendly, inexpensive place to stay for a few days. There were a series of gift shops and a gas station just 100-feet from the parking lot. Everyone involved with the Stardust was making money, but with owners and co-owners and hidden interests and the Mob all over Las Vegas, it was hard to tell who owned what. Licenses often named ten or more owners, but many of those were Los Angeles law firms just fronting for silent owners.

13 HOW TO GET A GAMING LICENSE

Obtaining a license to operate a casino was always an interesting task in early Nevada. When gaming was first legalized in 1931, a casino license was no tougher to get than a fishing license. Twenty years later it was a little tougher, and a lot more confusing. See if you can understand the Tax Commission's decisions here.

Jim McKay, Bill Graham, and Jack Sullivan, each owned a one-third interest in Reno's Bank Club. Sullivan was ready to retire. The partners chose Joseph "Doc" Stacher to purchase Sullivan's share and to work the club.

The Nevada Tax Commission held several hearings regarding Mr. Stacher's background, concerned about his circle of friends. When it was revealed that he was an associate of Lepke Buchalter of Murder, Inc., and other unsavory businessmen like Meyer Lansky, he was denied a license. Later, Doc was charged with conspiracy, gambling, and forgery involving gambling operations in New York. Six other defendants, including Meyer Lansky, were also charged in the Arrowhead Inn casino run at the Saratoga Spa and racetrack.

In a confidential report dated December 19, 1951, the Chicago Crime Commission stated that Joe Stacher had recently met with a large group of known gangsters at the Kenilworth Hotel in Hollywood, Florida. Abner "Longie" Zwillman was at the meeting, and he had recently purchased some property at Lake Tahoe. Stacher and Lansky were in close conversations, often joined by Moe Sedway.

When Stacher was charged in the Saratoga Spa fiasco, papers for extradition were transferred from New York to Nevada. Stacher, strangely enough, surrendered himself under the warrant in Las Vegas. He paid $5,000 cash bail, and a hearing was set for a week later.

Stacher, as many had learned, could move heaven and earth with enough money. He drove up to tiny Ely, Nevada, and before White Pine County Judge Harry Watson asked for the extradition order to be quashed. Watson had extra deputies placed on guard to make sure authorities didn't take Stacher to New York. The judge ruled Stacher was "Not a fugitive subject to extradition" and released him. Judge Watson had done a similar service for the Nevada Club's Lincoln Fitzgerald and Dan Sullivan before Nevada's governor stepped in and had the men extradited to Michigan. They paid a fine, and their casino ownership was never questioned in Nevada.

As with Fitzgerald, Stacher was eventually extradited to New York, but by then the wheels had been sufficiently greased. He was charged with twenty counts, pled guilty, paid a $10,000 fine, and was placed on two years' probation. This apparently made him respectable, so he moved to Las Vegas where he was licensed to open the Sands, and later the Fremont Hotel for Meyer Lansky's partners. Of course, that didn't help Jack Sullivan with his share of the Bank Club in Reno.

Unable to sell to Stacher, Graham and McKay purchased Sullivan's share and tried again to get the East Coast's interest into the club. This time they brought in David High, who ran a casino in New Jersey owned by Joe Adonis and Meyer Lansky, but swore he was just the restaurant manager. He was licensed to run the Golden Hotel, where the Bank Club was housed downstairs. What a restaurant manager knows about running a hotel was beside the point.

In February of 1952, the Golden Hotel was purchased for $6 million. The price included $3.5 million for McKay and Graham's interest in the casino. McKay retired, and Graham was awarded a new twenty-year lease for the entire downstairs, which had previously held both the Bank Club and the Golden Gulch Casino. Graham and High applied for a gaming license as the new Golden Bank Casino. Graham was quickly approved for licensing.

When David High was asked where he had gotten the money to purchase twenty-five percent of the casino, he told the state Tax Commission that Bill Graham had given him $500,000 after the sale of the Golden Hotel for his excellent work. Nice Boss! His application was denied.

Graham wound up with the license for 272 slot machines and 34 table games, as well as keno, pan, and a cabaret bar. With 40,000 square feet on one level, it was the largest casino in the world and took 400 employees to run.

The property was large; Bill Graham was old. Tony Accardo, in Chicago, suggested John Drew to "handle" things. Drew applied for a gaming license as a twenty-five percent owner of the Golden Bank Club Casino, for which he told the state he was paying $100,000.

Aside from the fact that the purchase price was suddenly just one-fifth what High said his twenty-five percent interest was worth, the state had other concerns and was reluctant to issue a license.

Drew had been arrested several times, including incidents where crooked dice were used to fleece victims in rigged crap games. Losses in those games were reported to have been as high as $250,000. He was also questioned regarding his association with Lester "Killer" Kruse.

First denying any association, Drew eventually admitted he was acquainted with him. Later, he admitted that he had hired him as a floor man in a casino. Drew stated he would have no interaction with Kruse, nor would Kruse have any interest in the club under his licensing.

Regarding the Golden Bank Club Casino, he denied he had any current connection to the club but had visited it a few times, so Commission Secretary Robbins Cahill and another member visited the club and asked a pit boss who was in charge. The pit boss took the men directly to John Drew.

When questioned about this strange occurrence, Drew suggested the pit boss must have been confused about the question put to him. The commission denied his license, but nothing lasts forever. Over the next month, Drew made the correct payments, reapplied, and was licensed for the same twenty-five percent he had been seeking earlier. To celebrate, Drew immediately hired old friend Lester "Killer" Kruse and made him a pit boss.

In December of 1955, John Drew and Bill Graham sold their interest in the casino and the remaining seventeen years on the lease for $425,000. Considering the previous owner had paid Graham, McKay, and High $4 million, this was the bargain of the century. The expanded, refurbished casino was now apparently worth only ten-percent of what it was just two years earlier. John Drew took his paltry $212,500 and bought five percent of Karat, Inc., the proposed Stardust casino operating company.

When the new Gaming Control Board questioned him about his frequent absences from the Bank Club and his many trips to Chicago, Drew said he would be more attentive to his new duties as the casino manager at the Stardust, which was a very good job. His application was approved.

14 WHAT'S UP WITH FRANKIE?

"What's up with Frankie?" Chicago boss Sam Giancana is heard asking on an FBI microphone "bug" placed inside the boss's favorite office. Maybe he was asking why Frank Sinatra hadn't been around much. Maybe he was asking why Sinatra was demanding more money to keep performing at the Sands casino where he already raked a share of the profits and was paid $100,000 a week. Hard to know for sure, but there is no doubt that Frank Sinatra considered his Mob friends his best buddies, and he tried hard never to let them down.

As for Giancana, he also had questions about the Cal-Neva Lodge that Frankie was licensed for, that he helped get a $1.75 million loan for, and that he owned half of. What Tony Accardo, boss of Chicago before and after Giancana took a turn running the Outfit was probably asking was, "What's up with Accardo?"

Back in 1948 when Sanford Adler and Charles Resnick were thrown out of the Flamingo Casino in Las Vegas, they headed to Reno, where they purchased the Fordonia Building from Jim McKay and Jack Sullivan, which housed the Club Fortune. Once the deal got finalized, Adler met again with McKay at the Bank Club, who directed him to Bones Remmer, to work out a deal for the Cal-Neva Lodge at Lake Tahoe. Although short of cash and friendless in Las Vegas, Adler was suddenly flush again and spent freely on the Cal-Neva.

He refurbished the entrance and built the resort's beautiful "Indian Room," and also had a massive fireplace constructed to grace the interior. A newly painted line down the California and Nevada border inside the building designated which state guests were standing in. Below the circular bar, which held breathtaking views of the Sierra Nevada Mountains and the crystal-clear lake, a similar line ran through the swimming pool, too.

The casino had several great summers, where craps and roulette were the favorite games of chance. Chuck-a-luck was also offered, as well as 21. However, Adler was still angry about being snubbed by the Nevada Tax Commission in 1948 and now refused to meet with the Gaming Control Board to answer questions about his partners. They yanked his license.

Getting a Mob boss to talk is like trying to crack walnuts made out of steel, as the Kefauver Committee found out. They had the right guys, but what did they learn? Not much. The same goes for the story behind the real owners of the Cal-Neva Lodge. They had connections to Lewis McWillie, who was sent by Johnny Roselli to watch over the Cal-Neva in 1961; Jack Ruby, who arrived at the Thunderbird Casino in Vegas to see McWillie and get "enough cash to pay off all the damn taxes," a week before he shot Lee Harvey Oswald; Sam Giancana, Frank Sinatra; both JFK and RFK; their father; Marilyn Monroe; the assassinations, the Castro/CIA/Chicago connection; the list goes on forever it seems, and it's well beyond this book about the Mob's ties to Las Vegas.

What is known (most of it also known by the FBI at the time), is that "Wingy" Grober came along to purchase the Lodge after Adler refused to meet with the Gaming Control Board and lost his gaming license. Wingy was a successful restaurateur with a short left arm and had a background in gaming. At least his friends did. In fact, when nearly every "heavy hitter" was in Havana for a conference with the deported Lucky Luciano, so was Wingy. His old friend and liquor supplier, Joe Kennedy, visited the Cal-Neva often. Sources now indicate that Grober may well have been a front for Kennedy, both in the earlier restaurants and at the Lodge.

Visitors to the Lodge included Frank Sinatra, Robert Kennedy and his wife, Ethel, Teddy Kennedy, Peter Lawford and his wife, Patricia Kennedy, Dean Martin, and again, the list goes on. It is also possible that Peter Lawford, Dean Martin, Frank Sinatra and Joe Kennedy may have been planning to purchase the property and do so publicly.

Sinatra, always comfortable around celebrities and politicians, was equally comfortable, almost eagerly solicitous, of mobsters. He counted as friends people like Carlo Gambino, Tony Accardo, Sam Giancana and Willie Moretti, who some swore got him out of his contract with band leader Tommy Dorsey by forcing a gun down his throat.

Whether that was true or not, William F. Roemer, Jr., FBI Special Agent who had access in Chicago to microphones all over town, repeatedly heard about Sinatra and the Cal-Neva Lodge directly from Sam Giancana. One microphone dubbed "Little Al," picked-up detailed conversations and helped the FBI piece things together.

Joe Kennedy, eager to have son John F. Kennedy elected to the presidency of the United States, solicited help from all comers, including Frank Sinatra, and Giancana. Paul "Skinny" D'Amato, the manager of the Atlantic 500 Club, took some friends to West Virginia, where Kennedy desperately needed a win in the primary. There, they passed out cash to tavern owners, supposedly to play Sinatra's reworked version of his previous hit, "High Hopes," over and over each day (the tune had different lyrics and was used as the theme song for the 1960 Presidential Campaign of John Kennedy) on their jukeboxes. You know, "Here's $1000, just keep playing the 5-cent song." Joe Kennedy spent $1.5 million in the state compared to Hubert Humphrey's $25,000. Kennedy won by a 60-40 margin. Humphrey said later, "Well, I don't have a bag of money to take all over the state."

Sinatra promised Joe Kennedy that Giancana would help "set" the election, and in return, the government (read: J. Edgar Hoover's FBI via Robert Kennedy) would be persuaded to back off their pressure on the Chicago Outfit. JFK, of course, won the election. RFK, as U.S. Attorney General, did not back off pressure on organized crime. Giancana was pissed-off and blamed Sinatra.

When "Wingy" Grober suddenly decided to sell "his" Cal-Neva Lodge for the bargain price of just $250,000, there was no longer even the slightest doubt that outside owners had control of the Cal-Neva. Dean Martin, who had planned to get licensed with Frank Sinatra, suddenly got cold feet when he heard who his partners would be, and dropped out of the deal.

Sinatra was his usual blustery, confident self, and went about rebuilding much of the Lodge, expanding it, and putting in the elegant Celebrity Room, all with the $1.75 million loan Giancana arranged. His plans included some "necessary" items, like a helicopter pad on the roof.

Sinatra also built a pad at his home in Palm Springs; planning to fly easily between the two spots and a new "super resort" he wanted to build in Reno. The helicopter pads were also an enticement to get new president John F. Kennedy to visit. He did.

Sinatra was able to convince plenty of Hollywood friends to come to the Cal-Neva, and he filled the showroom with stars such as Trini Lopez, Buddy Rich, Tony Bennett, and the McGuire Sisters. Phyllis McGuire was dating Sam Giancana at the time. Sinatra was trying to have an affair with Marilyn Monroe. Both John F. Kennedy and his brother, Robert, had also been involved with Marilyn. It was a healthy situation.

Sinatra had several tunnels expanded under the lodge. One ran from the closet of his cabin to the main tunnel, which had access to the back of the lodge, and to two other cabins. Only special guests like Sam Giancana, J.F.K., Marilyn Monroe, and a new lady who was also sleeping with both John F. Kennedy and Giancana, named Judy Campbell, were issued the cabins with tunnel access. Giancana preferred lodge 50 when he stayed at the resort, his resort. The FBI was following Campbell, and documents show that at one point in Chicago she was with both the President and Giancana on subsequent days.

Also in the tunnels beneath the casino, Sinatra built a room for himself, completely encased in steel. He wanted to feel safe while he was cooking the books.

Marilyn was going through a break-up with her husband, Arthur Miller at the time. She was less spunky than the cinema queen who had once so glibly explained her nude Playboy magazine photos and toyed with the press so effortlessly once was. At that time, Monroe did some interviews, and when a journalist asked what she had on during the photo-shoot, she replied, "the radio." When asked what she wore to bed, she said, "Channel Number 5," and cultivated a world full of fans and admirers.

By the summer of 1960, her life was a daily torture. She couldn't sleep without pills, and she couldn't work before noon. She and Clark Gable were in Reno filming the movie, *The Misfits* when Frank invited the entire crew up to the Cal-Neva to see his show. The film would be the last for both Gable and Monroe.

Sam Giancana was happy with the arrangement for the Cal-Neva Lodge. He had guaranteed the electoral-rich state of Illinois in the election of Kennedy and was now reaping the benefits. In his mind, he was "getting half of the Cal-Neva for nothing." Paul D'Amato took care of the money, and everyone was happy

D'Amato was also running a large prostitution ring from the bell desk at the lodge. Hookers from the San Francisco Bay Area were brought up to the lake regularly to entertain guests. The casino was making plenty of money, and Sinatra was happy with his cut of the pie. However, instead of a governmental relaxation of the pressure on organized crime and Giancana, the opposite was happening.

When Giancana realized that Sinatra couldn't deliver on his promises he started pushing harder for Frank to do something. Perhaps, Giancana realized, Frankie wasn't as close and influential with the new President as he had promised he would be.

Robert F. Kennedy had been a thorn in organized crime's side for ten years already. He started working for the United States Department of Justice in 1951. In 1952, he became an assistant counsel for the Senate Permanent Subcommittee on Investigations, and later was chief counsel for the Senate Labor Rackets Committee.

He had been very tough on Jimmy Hoffa, the Teamsters Union President, who would eventually be convicted of attempted bribery of a grand juror, and sentenced to a jail term of thirteen years. Giancana and the rest of the organized families across the U.S. were less than pleased when Robert Kennedy became the United States Attorney General after John's election to the Presidency. Some movies have portrayed him as too young, and ineffective, but history, and secret FBI wires and "bugs" have borne out the opposite.

Robert F. Kennedy was now even more vigilant against organized crime than he had been before his brother was elected, and Giancana felt betrayed by both Joe Kennedy, and Sinatra. During the new Attorney General's term, convictions against notorious organized crime figures rose 800%. Strangely enough, his policies and strategies were often found to clash with J. Edgar Hoover.

Hoover's "bugs" routinely picked up reams of data, but little seemed ever to come of the information. As early as 1944, Hoover's men were watching Bugsy Siegel and listening in on conversations at his home, in hotel rooms at the Flamingo, at the St. Francis Hotel in San Francisco, and in his Las Vegas Club casino offices – as well as following his every step around the country. However, they seemed woefully unaware of what was transpiring at the Flamingo construction site, the casino after it was built, or that he was the target of a coming Mob hit. If they were aware, they never shared.

In Reno, fighter Jack Dempsey was a subject of surveillance. In 1953, according to official memorandums from the SAC Salt Lake City, to Hoover, Dempsey "Stayed at the Golden Hotel, and is an old friend of William Graham, who is the owner of the gaming concessions of the establishment, and who made a chorus girl available for Dempsey's pleasure."

The strange thing about this report is that the FBI is aware of Bill Graham but is not watching him, they are watching Dempsey. At the same time, John Drew was also on the property, sent by Tony Accardo from Chicago. Even the state of Nevada had a problem with him, until caving for whatever reason and allowing his purchase of a 25% stake in the casino, but hey, let's watch the ex-boxing champ and the chorus girl.

Frank Sinatra, trying very hard to hold on to his relationship with the Kennedy's, and Giancana, was also pursuing Monroe, for whom he purchased a puppy. With her usual sense of humor and fun, she called the dog Maf, short for Mafia. She also confided to a friend, "Sure, the men like the sex part, but I don't understand what all the fuss is about."

Regardless of the behind-the-scenes machinations, players, tourists, and locals headed to the Cal-Neva Lodge in droves. The casino was constantly busy, and stars were seen above the lake, as well as in the restaurant and showroom. Even Virginia Hill was seen playing craps with friends from Chicago at the Cal-Neva in Lake Tahoe!

After Bugsy Siegel's death in 1947, Virginia Hill moved to Sun Valley, Idaho and had a home in Washington. She traveled to Reno on several occasions and stayed at the Mapes in Reno. She was convicted of income tax evasion in 1954 and later moved to Europe. She died of an overdose of sleeping pills in Koppl, near Salzburg, Austria on March 24, 1966. She was 49.

Sinatra also held a gaming license at the Sands in Las Vegas, and his nine-percent paid him handsomely. He got a taste of the Dunes profits too, gratis. He routinely snubbed the state's gaming agents and assumed he was invincible, although he and Dean Martin were forced to sell their holdings in the Berkshire Downs racetrack in Massachusetts. They were directors of the track, and other owners included New England Mafia boss, Gaetano Lucchese, the head of one of New York's five families.

Near the end of June of 1962, D'Amato's prostitution ring began to unravel. The FBI was there to investigate, and an agent ran into one of Giancana's men, Chuckie English, who was drunk, and told him, "If Bobby (Robert) Kennedy wants to know anything about Momo (Giancana), all he has to do is ask Sinatra."

A few days later, the club experienced its second attempted murder of the year when an employee of the Cal-Neva was shot outside the front doors in the valet area. Neither "hit" resulted in death, but both were successful in that neither man ever talked about the incident again.

The following day, Sinatra was told by Deputy Sheriff Richard

Anderson to stay away from his wife, who worked at the Lodge as a waitress. She had previously dated Sinatra before marrying Anderson, and the friction was like two blocks of sandpaper rubbing together.

The two men ran into each other again in the restaurant's kitchen later in the week. Sinatra stormed up to Anderson and demanded to know what he was doing there.

"This is for employees only, what the fuck are you doing here?"

"Just waiting for my wife, Frankie," said Anderson. "Mr. Sinatra, it's Mr. Sinatra, you fucking ass," Frank said, as he tried to remove the much larger Anderson.

In the ensuing scuffle, Anderson popped Sinatra in the mouth hard enough to keep him off the stage for a week. On July 17, Anderson and his wife were driving down the mountain on Highway 28 near the Cal-Neva when Richard noticed a new convertible bearing down on them at an excessive speed.

"What the hell is this joker doing?" Anderson asked. Before his wife could reply, the maroon sports car closed in on them and sideswiped their vehicle. The impact forced Anderson and his wife off the road where the car fishtailed before striking a tree. Both were badly injured in the crash. Richard died before reaching the hospital.

At the end of the month, Sinatra talked Marilyn Monroe into coming up to the lake again. She was reluctant, but he promised Robert Kennedy would be there, and she changed her mind. Frank arranged to have her flown up for the week, and the second night she had dinner with Peter and Pat Lawford, Sam Giancana, and her host, Sinatra. During the dinner show, Marilyn had just two drinks but became heavily intoxicated and violently ill. She was escorted back to her room where she passed out on the bed.

Conversations picked up by the microphone "Little Al," in Chicago, later revealed that not only did her escort, Giancana, have sex with her while she was passed out, but so did several other male and female "friends," allowed into the room. Sinatra was in the room at the time when photographs were taken. The film made its way to Hollywood photographer Billy Woodfield, who developed the pictures. Then the pictures made their way to Robert Kennedy, who told Peter Lawford to tell Monroe that he did not want to ever have any contact with her again. When she protested, Lawford showed her two of the photos. She continued trying to see Robert, but whether she ever did is unknown.

The emotionally distraught starlet died a week later at her home in Brentwood, California. Strangely enough, there is a four-hour gap between the time her body was discovered (meaning the time of death) and the time the first phone call to the Los Angeles Police Department was made. The first officer on the scene claimed it looked as though her body had been "posed." When he arrived, the live-in maid was doing the laundry.

Friend Peter Lawford, Kennedy's brother-in-law, said he talked to her earlier on the phone and she "Sounded groggy like she was taking sleeping pills." However, there were no signs of a drug overdose, and the autopsy showed no trace of the barbiturates Monroe often used to get to sleep, in her mouth, stomach or intestines. There were no bottles of pills or drugs in her room or house. What was present was lividity, a settling of the blood, in various parts of the body, which strongly suggests that the body had been moved after death.

Certainly, questions remain about her tragic death. Peter Lawford's home was nearby and offered a convenient rendezvous spot for friends and lovers, but he offered the alibi that she was at home and talking to him on the phone when she died. FBI documents show Robert Kennedy was staying in Gilroy, California at the time, about a four-hour drive away. The FBI was aware of her situation at Lake Tahoe, and government officials were certainly uncomfortable with the fact that she had a relationship with the Kennedy brothers and also knew Giancana.

Some also believe that Giancana could have been involved in her death, as a way of "pushing" the Kennedy administration into backing off their pursuit of the Mob. Again, the Mob felt betrayed by the Kennedy's. JFK had written a personal note to Sinatra before the election that said, "Frank – How much can I count on from the boys in Vegas? JFK." Norman Biltz worked hard for Kennedy, collecting nearly $15 million in the state, virtually all of it from the Las Vegas casino owners, for the Kennedy war chest. But what had they gotten in return? Nada.

The Cal-Neva continued making money, and Sinatra provided star power for Giancana's Villa Venice Supper Club in Wheeling, Illinois. Picked up on phone taps, it was obvious that Frankie was helping Giancana for some reason, as the stars who appeared November 9, 1962, all worked for free. The bill that evening included Eddie Fisher, who opened the festivities; Sammy Davis Jr. who sang and danced for the well-heeled crowd; Dean Martin, who joked and sang; and finally the headliner, Frank Sinatra.

Guests attending the show were then shuttled a few blocks to an ugly warehouse facility surrounded by rusting car parts. Inside the warehouse was a plush casino. Revenue for the evening was over $1.2 million dollars.

The FBI, as usual, provided little information to other authorities, and Sam Giancana was a welcome guest of Sinatra's at the Lodge for another year. Eventually, the FBI did provide information to the State Gaming Control Board after Giancana was involved in a fight at the Cal-Neva.

Ed Olsen, the Gaming Control Board's Chairman, sent two investigators to the Lodge and got an interesting response. They were told, "Don't worry about it, nothing's happening," and one of the agents had a $100 bill tucked into his pocket.

Olsen talked to his agents, and then called the General Manager, Paul D'Amato. He was unavailable, so a message was left. The following day, Sinatra was the one who returned the call. He was told that between the dates of July 17 and July 28, 1963, Sam Giancana was in use of the facilities at the Cal-Neva Lodge with the knowledge and consent of the licensee.

Sinatra never denied the charge, but he did ask Olsen to come up to the lake from his offices in Carson City so they could talk. Olsen declined the offer, and Sinatra flew into a rage.

"You're acting like a fucking cop, I just want to talk to you off the record," Sinatra said.

Now Olsen took offense. Frank was told in no uncertain terms that it would be better for all parties involved if he concentrated on his enterprises elsewhere.

"Don't fuck with me, I don't take this shit from anyone else, and I'm not going to take it from you, a pencil-pushing cock sucker," sputtered Sinatra.

Then, thinking better of his statements, he again asked Olsen to come up to the lake. Olsen told Sinatra that he was setting a formal hearing date for October 7 in Carson City.

Grant Sawyer, the governor of Nevada, received several telephone calls from people who talked about their ability to supply large contributions for his coming election campaign. They also expressed hope that Mr. Sinatra's problems could be resolved amicably. Sawyer refused the campaign funds.

Both Sawyer and Olsen were very much interested in finding out how much money was leaving the casinos as skim but were severely stymied by a portion of the Nevada Gaming Control Act which guaranteed casino owners that their financial data would not be disclosed. What an amazing law the state allowed the casinos to use to steal. Sawyer was defeated for reelection.

After the Gaming Control Board had met with Sinatra, he read a statement to the press. It outlined how he had decided to devote more of his time to the entertainment industry, and that he would divest himself completely from any involvement in the Nevada gaming industry. The board gave him ninety-days to sell his casino holdings.

15 HOWARD HUGHES

Howard Hughes was a regular visitor to Nevada, buying land here and there, but his casino purchases in the late 1960s changed the way Nevada looked to the rest of the world, and they made it tougher for the Mob to skim money. Not impossible, but tougher.

Howard Robard Hughes, Jr. was born on Christmas Eve, 1905. At the time, his parents, Allene and Howard Hughes, were like many other couples starting out their lives together. Allene worked hard to keep the wood floors of their Crawford Street home clean and free of mud. Cooking took a great deal of time, and she often shopped due to an aversion to canning. The porch out front was the only cool spot during the hot summer, but the winters were cold. The house was rented and small, but it still took plenty of wood to keep it heated. Insulation was rarely used in clapboard houses.

Both Allene and Howard were well educated. "Big Howard" earned a business degree from Harvard and a law degree from Iowa State. He was a spirited and inquisitive man, but the law business was a bore to him, and they moved to their home in Houston to allow "Big Howard" to try his hand at land and oil leasing. In 1907, Howard and a friend built and patented a new style of the drill bit for oil exploration. A year later they formed the Sharp-Hughes Tool Company.

The drills were a big hit, and by the time Mr. Sharp died in 1917, the company was the most successful in the field. Howard purchased the Sharp family interests for $325,000.

Allene Hughes died at a young age in 1922, and Big Howard succumbed to heart problems just two years later. Young Howard was left alone at the tender age of 19 but was ready to take over the business. He convinced his relatives to sell their interest in the Hughes Tool Company for all the cash the business had in the bank: $300,000. Then he hired Noah Dietrich to handle all those messy details involved in actually running the business.

Over the years, Hughes distinguished himself as both an aviator, and an innovator, but he was no businessman. As a fearless flyer, he set many speed records, including a new land-plane speed in 1935 of 353 MPH, a full 40 miles per hour faster than the previous record. He also established a new coast-to-coast record of nine hours and 27 minutes and established record times between New York and Miami, and Chicago and Los Angeles. In 1937 he won the Harmon Trophy for his contributions to air progress.

His record in the movie business was less stellar, but he did sign some big stars like Jane Russell, and she made several popular movies, including *The Las Vegas Story*. His ventures into RKO Pictures keep his name in the public eye and so did the building of the Hughes Flying Boat.

Officially named the HK-1 or Hercules, the Spruce Goose was large enough to carry 700 people. A 747 carries 490 passengers. Although the HK-1 made only a few short flights before it took up permanent residence in the Long Beach Harbor, it cost Hughes $50 million dollars of his own money to develop and build.

In the early 1950s, he purchased large plots of land in Las Vegas, determined not to be left out of the great expansion he saw coming to Nevada. In 1953, he bought what became known as the Husite property. He spoke at the time of moving all his Hughes Aircraft operations to Nevada, and it wasn't just a smoke screen that he often employed, he was honestly considering a permanent move to Las Vegas because Nevada offered him something California and Texas couldn't: a tax haven. Howard hated taxes more than germs, and the State of Nevada had no personal income tax.

In 1957, Noah Dietrich severed his ties to Hughes over a stock option plan he had been promised for years, but that somehow never developed. Howard felt that familiar pain of being alone, so the next week he took Jean Peters to Tonopah, and they were wed in a secret civil marriage. Jean tried to keep him active, but he was too ill-at-ease socially, and it was Jean Peters who had to change. She remained a part-time wife throughout their marriage, and she spent most of her time alone at the new home he purchased for her in Southern California. Then, Howard hired a new man to oversee his Nevada operations. A man with serious "spy-ties" named Robert Maheu.

The thought of having Hughes move all of the Hughes enterprises to Nevada was of great interest to the locals in Las Vegas, but it was thirteen years before he made any appreciable impact. By that time the Husite property was worth approximately $25 million dollars, a pretty good increase for a $62,000 original investment.

After ten years of plotting, publicity, and failed propaganda, Howard Hughes finally made his big move to Las Vegas on Thanksgiving Day November 24, 1966. Howard had been hiding from tax men, movie studio managers, his wife, his girlfriends, and himself for so long his real self was lost. When he arrived in Sin City, he was a recluse who had not been seen in public for nearly ten years. He was also a man with a lot of cash on his books. When Hughes was forced to sell-off his 70 percent stake in TWA, the stock was at $86 per share. The huge cash bonanza provided by the sale of his TWA stock that had been selling at just $13 per share when he lost control of the company in 1960 left him with nearly $450 million dollars, and Howard came to Las Vegas to spend it.

Hank Greenspun, the wily and combative publisher of the Las Vegas Sun, had regular conversations with Hughes, even while he was holed-up in the projection room of his offices in Los Angeles for months at a time. At some point, Hank was asked to help make reservations for the invisible tycoon at one of the luxury hotels on the strip. His first try was at the Dunes, but their management wouldn't allocate the amount of space he needed. So, Greenspun tried the Desert Inn, where he reserved the entire ninth-floor and penthouse for Hughes and his entourage.

By this time Robert A. Maheu was in charge of most of the millionaire's operations. He wasn't running the company; he was a business associate who knew how to get things done. Maheu was a former FBI agent and counterspy who had a lot of friends and contacts, and he spent over a month at the Desert Inn before Hughes finally arrived. However, even after Hughes' special train had pulled into Union Plaza and unloaded the frail-looking older gentleman on a stretcher, Maheu hadn't personally met with him. In all the time they worked together, it was never in person!

Howard's mind was sharp at times, but sometimes he fretted and stressed over the simplest things. He didn't want to be seen by anyone, so he sealed himself within the penthouse of the Desert Inn like a ghost. He had specialty black-out drapes made to block the sun and those pesky neon lights that went winking and blinking into the night. After a week he had no desire to leave, but the casino needed the rooms for use by their high-rollers during the New Year's week and would need the space for their golf tournaments.

Maheu offered to double the cost of the two floors that Howard was paying (a hefty $26,000 a day). The hotel manager refused. "Tell them were staying anyway," Howard told Maheu, who placed a call to Johnny Roselli, who bought the millionaire a little more time in the hotel.

The next week it was Moe Dalitz that Maheu was dealing with, and Moe wasn't happy. Without those rooms, the Desert Inn's big New Year's Eve party was going to be a bust. He demanded that Hughes get out. Maheu smiled and returned to the penthouse where he was allowed into the outer room where Howard's Morman Mafia, as his Mormon aides were being called, remained at Howard's beck and call, outside his bedroom suite. Inside, Howard was injecting himself with codeine on such a regular basis that both of his arms now had more than a dozen broken needles embedded permanently in them.

Still, Howard smiled when he was given the news. "That damn Moe, I know about Kleinman, I know about Hoffa, I know about the Purple men (Purple Gang), Howard said to Mahue over a phone line that stretched just 30-feet from one room to the other. Tell him I'll buy his little hotel," Howard said. Maheu returned downstairs and met with Dalitz, in person, at the bar.

Maheu wasn't cagey, nor did he like to beat around the bush. "How would you feel about selling the Desert Inn, Mr. Dalitz?" he asked. Now it was Moe's turn to smile, but he was confused. He'd never considered selling before. "I'm always interested in negotiating," he said.

No matter how good a negotiator Moe thought he was, he had met his match in Howard Hughes. Not because Hughes drove a hard bargain, but because Hughes second-guessed himself every ten minutes. Once the men got in the same ballpark, price-wise, Howard demanded some concessions. Moe relinquished none initially but caved to later demands. Eventually, an agreement was ready for lawyers, so Howard changed the wording and transfer details. When Moe agreed, he demanded another dozen changes be made. Howard wanted the deal to be consummated at 7 pm, then at 6 pm, then midnight. Moe refused.

Howard sat up each night writing notes to Mahue, his aides, Jean Peters (yup, still married), and then changed them over and over each afternoon. Once the lawyers got the papers, Howard still wanted to make more changes. Eventually, the paperwork was done and sent back to Howard.

When the papers made their way to Dalitz again, he was ready to sign, but still, Howard wasn't. He wanted to make a few more changes. Dalitz confided to his partner, Roen, "I'm ready to shoot the old fool." He might have felt differently if he had seen Hughes in person. He was much peppier after being involved in some business negotiations again, but his gray hair hung in his face and tangled in his beard. He wasn't eating, so he looked like a concentration camp survivor. And the smell. Who could stand his breath? He last had a shave and haircut six months earlier. And, he refused his monthly enema; the only way to relieve his constipation caused by the codeine, although the one person allowed to perform the procedure was billing by the hour and had been at the hotel for a week.

On March 22, 1967, the D. I. negotiations ended with a purchase price of $13.2 million to be paid by Howard for the land and the buildings. Present at the meeting were Hughes's representatives including Maheu and D. I. officials Moe Dalitz, Maurice Kleinman, and Jack Donnelley. The transfer of casino ownership in Nevada is a long and arduous affair unless you are Howard Hughes.

In this case, Howard gave his power of attorney to Richard Gray and had the license put in the name of Hughes Tool Company to avoid ever coming face to face with any Gaming Control Board members. All anybody knew at that time was that Hughes was 61 years old, listed at six-foot-two, 150 pounds, and was self-employed, maybe. Of course, for all anybody knew, he could also be dead.

That was good enough for the Nevada Gaming Commission and the Clark County Licensing Board, which unanimously approved the necessary local license to become effective at 12:01 AM, April 1, 1967. There was no official count done at the casino cage, and it is impossible to know how much cash walked out the door with Moe Dalitz. It is also impossible to know how much money was removed from Hughes's properties over the years through skim.

It was a fantastic deal for the crime families across the nation that had a piece of any number of Las Vegas clubs. They were able to sell their casinos at an inflated price, and still take a rake-off from an unseen owner! Maheu, being a former FBI agent, saw skeletons in every closet and set about improving security at each of the Hughes properties, but that didn't keep them from bleeding cash.

Still, Howard was happy, and a happy guy with all the money in the world likes to play with things, so the Howard Hughes buying spree was just beginning. In July of 1967, Maheu and his contacts in the Mob make a deal for the Sands. Frank Sinatra was less than happy with the sale. He had been a part-owner since the management group came up with the idea that Frank would entertain at the club if he owned a piece. His ownership gave him a lot of power around the property.

Years earlier Hughes had inquired about several casinos that were on his radar but refused to consider the Cal-Neva Lodge at North Shore when the Nevada Gaming Board forced Sinatra out. He had talked to Bill Harrah too, about his Lake Tahoe casino, and looked into buying Harold's Club in Reno because they were listed as the two top earners in the state in 1960, but Sinatra's Lodge was not on his list of properties to purchase.

Frank may have been off the official papers at the Sands, but he still appeared in the showroom, and he and his Rat Pack were a welcome sight at any casino they happened to wander into in Las

Vegas. Sammy Davis, Jr., Dean Martin, Peter Lawford, and Joey Bishop made quite a group. They all drank, they all gambled, they all drew stares, photos, and publicity. Sometimes the Rat Pack Mascots were in town, including Angie Dickinson, Juliet Prowse, and Shirley MacLaine. Outside on the Sands marquee, the headline read, "DEAN MARTIN - MAYBE FRANK - MAYBE SAMMY" Fans adored them. Casino personnel were a little cooler to their antics.

When Frank was at the Sands gambling, he'd often get chips on-the-sleeve (no paperwork) to double down on a bet. If he won, he'd pay the bet back. If he lost, he'd walk away, off the hook for any cash. He also made plenty of demands at the cage. "Look," he'd say, "if I can't get another $50,000 I may have to consider doing my show elsewhere."

When that happened, a manager usually signed for the free loan, and Sinatra never paid a dime of it back. One week he had already been to the cage twice, and when he demanded more money, he was denied. He was playing 21 and pounded the table, so hard chips flew out of the tray and onto the floor. Frank was anything but quiet.

He berated the dealer, he pushed the cocktail server away, and he told the pit boss, "Listen, you're never working in this town again." The pit boss had already been told that Mr. Sinatra was done, no more money, so he stood his ground. Sinatra screamed at him again and then grabbed the railing of the 21 table and nearly turned it over. Again, chips rained to the floor, but the pit boss never moved. Sinatra stormed across the casino, his face twitching, searching for Carl Cohen, the Casino Manager.

When he found him in the coffee shop, Sinatra grabbed his table, but couldn't pick it up because it was bolted to the floor. He did manage to spill Cohen's coffee cup. The 55-year-old Cohen looked at Sinatra for a moment and then rose from his chair. When he got to his feet, he plastered Sinatra in the mouth, knocking out two front teeth and leaving him with a bloody nose.

Sinatra was quoted later as saying, "They wouldn't give me any credit in the casino, and I don't know what the problem was." Sinatra was probably more concerned with the $14.6 million sale of the Sands. Meyer Lansky and others would be getting their fair share of the sales price, but Sinatra would receive less than he felt was right, and the night's events proved that he had lost all his "juice."

The Sands did fine without Sinatra and the Rat Pack, but other changes weren't as popular with locals or tourists. Hughes sat in his room, ignored his three-inch fingernails, and made long lists of changes for Maheu to make at the casinos, one of which was to stop the use of call girls for "high-rollers." Chorus girls were no longer expected to sit around the lounges for an hour after their shows. Governor Laxalt stated, "You're never going to eliminate the girls," but it was the beginning of the upgrading of Las Vegas.

After that point, if a high roller wanted a girl sent to his room, he had to get his "host" to take care of it, or he could always check with the Bell Captain. Guys at the bell desk always seemed to know what was going on in town and how to score whatever was needed. The city now had what amounted to corporate ownership of several casinos. What a concept. If they could only have seen who owned the properties!

It was also the time of the Weekend Warriors, who showed up late Friday night and left Sunday evening. Most of the warriors were young ladies from Southern California. Imagine being a 26-year old kindergarten teacher in Pasadena and trying to live on $4,800 a year in teacher pay.

Imagine also that perhaps in Las Vegas, nobody will know you, and you can meet a few men on Friday and Saturday, maybe get $20 from each one and make $100 for the weekend. The ladies hit the casinos, walked the clubs in miniskirts, and flirted with the men who had plenty of chips. What's a green chip anyway? $25 bucks? Some warriors were so good at their jobs that a weekend was worth two or three hundred dollars, tripling their annual income.

Others were happy with a few "dates," and maybe $50 for an all-nighter on Saturday evening, because a girl's gotta' do what a girl's gotta' do, and why pay for your hotel room? All Howard's new rules did was open up the chip hustling and whoring to a new band of ladies, and soon the best ones didn't have to drive, they flew into town on $19 flights!

As for Howard, he hadn't been on a plane for a decade. He was an addled old man, shut off from the real world, and he spent the bulk of his time watching TV from his recliner and writing notes to

Maheu. His toenails were growing to amazing lengths, and they twisted in impossible directions. His feet no longer fit in the Kleenex boxes he wore as slippers years earlier, but it wasn't necessary to ever leave his room, as far as he was concerned.

For meals, his aides brought him cooked strips of chicken that might have already been reheated four or five times during the evening before he managed to choke down a few ounces. He drank milk, and dishes of fruit from cans were prepared for him in a very special way.

Howard slaved for a week over a six-page manuscript, explaining how each can be cleaned and re-cleaned before opening. Then, the label was removed, and the can was again cleaned under a running tap before it was opened. The aid doing the opening had already gone through a ritual of hand washing that rivaled any heart surgeon's pre-operative scrub. Finally, the fruit was brought to Hughes in a clean, white-only dish, and set down by his bed so he could ignore it. Along the wall, Howard lined milk bottle after milk bottle of his urine. His mind was now mush.

Hughes was intent on making Las Vegas his ideal community. He announced a super "city with-in a city" expansion at the Sands. His new casinos were already taking advantage of computers, and tracking action on each table. The new Sands would be 4000 rooms with electronically coded credit card door locks. He promised 24-hour shops, a motion picture theater, and a "family fun area." The idea of a family theme was still new to Las Vegas. Hughes spoke of recreation that would include the world's largest bowling alley, a poolroom and ice-skating. Rooms would also have chess, bridge, ski-ball and table tennis. His idea was to provide a complete vacation and pleasure complex anywhere in the world. Of course, Las Vegas already was for most men. They didn't want chess boards; they wanted the hookers back.

Howard's plans usually stayed on the drawing table, because he compulsively changed and re-changed every detail over and over again. His need to make things perfect doomed him to doing absolutely nothing. He was unable to do things halfway, and he couldn't seem to get anything just right so it could be implemented. Corporate boardrooms often have these problems as board members squabble with each other, Howard argued with himself. With him, it was his own mind and ego that were fighting, although he did like to fight constantly with Robert Maheu, too.

Hughes continued purchasing casinos at an astonishing rate. He had almost no input on the way they were run, and each managed to lose a substantial amount of money. Maheu retained most of the "old crew" of bosses at each property. He was a friend of Johnny Roselli, and it was Jimmy "the Weasel" Fratianno who stated that Roselli told him the whole DI purchase was a mob set-up. He said they talked Hughes into purchasing the property, and continued skimming the profits.

Strangely enough, Maheu also worked for the CIA in the late 1950s, before Howard Hughes hired him. In 1960, the CIA told him to approach Johnny Roselli about a plot to kill Fidel Castro. Although he offered to forward $150,000 to have Castro killed, Roselli declined the cash, ready to work for free, because he and many other Mob families had taken such a financial beating when Castro shut down Cuba's casinos. According to FBI documents, Roselli introduced Maheu to "Sam" and "Joe," who turned out to be Sam Giancana and Santo Trafficante, Jr. and Operation Mongoose was underway. Years later, Maheu would say that working for the CIA and FBI was easy compared to working for Howard Hughes.

Hughes made the nation think Las Vegas was now clean, but the IRS would later say that Hughes had been the victim of a vast Mob skim topping $50 million.

Hughes went blissfully on making purchases. The Frontier Casino was next, purchased for $14 million from the R. & H. Holding Company. Irving Leff, T. Warner Richardson, Maurice Friedman, Beldon Katleman, B. Frank Williams, and Jack Barenfield headed the group. The Frontier also had ties to "Eastern groups." Those ties included stockholders listed in hotel memos as Anthony J. Zerilli, the President of Detroit's Hazel Park Racetrack, Attorney Pete Bellance, Jack Dean, and Louis Elias.

Their involvement in the casino was never proved, and Hughes took over on Sept. 22, 1967. The casino was quite small but included ten craps tables, twenty blackjack games, two roulette wheels, one baccarat table, and a hundred-seat keno lounge and slots. It was not enough to keep the new Hughes team busy. The Castaway's came next.

Hughes paid $3 million for the 230-room Castaway's hotel-casino, which had begun life as the Sans Souci. The name change was made by a group of investors headed by Ike P. LaRue, of Jackson, Mississippi. Remodeling took up too much of the group's cash, and they ran the club for only three months. Oliver M. Kahle was the owner of record when Hughes took over.

The Silver Slipper also became a Hughes' property on May 1, 1968, when he paid $5.3 million for it. It was a very important purchase for Hughes, because the "Stupid revolving slipper" was too bright for his room, even with the blackout curtains. Plus, Howard was certain the FBI was taking pictures of him from the toe of the shoe. For some reason, it stopped each revolution while pointed right at his penthouse.

The price was high, but Hughes didn't care. Soon the Silver Slipper became a free ATM for Nevada politicians, as $858,500 was drawn from the cage of the small club and given away. There was nothing improper about the contributions, but the payments were always made in cash, and the politicians never signed a receipt. How much of this slush fund went to political campaigning costs is impossible to say, but the reader should think small.

Hughes bought the Landmark construction site next. The Landmark was started in November of 1961, but the owners ran out of money (did nobody in Vegas ever hire a consulting team before breaking ground?), so the project sat stalled for six years. As usual, Howard's ego got the best of him as he competed with Kirk Kerkorian to build the tallest structure in Nevada in 1969.

Kerkorian, like Hughes, was an aviation buff, skilled flyer, and owned a small airline company. He first visited Las Vegas in 1944 and enjoyed gambling, but quit after purchasing Trans International Airlines in 1947 for $60,000. The small air-charter service had contracts with several hotels and flew gamblers from the Los Angeles area into Las Vegas.

Also like Hughes, Kerkorian began purchasing land in the area, and the 80 acres he purchased across the Strip from the Flamingo for $960,000 was eventually developed for Caesars Palace. He sold the land in 1968 for over $8 million.

The year before, Kerkorian began construction of the International Hotel on 82 acres along Paradise Road. His hotel was slated to open the same weekend as the Howard Hughes Landmark casino. It was also expected to be slightly taller than the Landmark, which made Howard even crazier if that was possible. Kerkorian hired and trusted a construction firm, foreman, and architectural firm to finish his resort. Howard was in semi-control of the Landmark. He wrote notes; he changed the interior decorator; he changed the lighting scheme for the roof, and he tried to make the building taller.

For Robert Maheu, it seemed as though the property would never open. Howard spent three weeks making out a list of everybody that should be invited to the gala grand opening. But as the days dragged on, Howard continued to change the list. He made a list of fifty businessmen and sent it to Maheu, only to send a revision two hours later.

After fifteen days, the list had ballooned to 350 people, only to be whittled down to three by the 25th of June. Howard, down to just 110 pounds and using more injections of codeine to relieve the pain of his infected gums, pressed on by changing the plans daily. Maheu sat in his Las Vegas home not 500-yards from the Desert Inn and drank heavily. He and Howard talked on the phone constantly.

Eventually, Maheu decided on his own agenda, and the casino opened in July of 1969 with a tiny party that didn't even have a caterer until just six hours before it started. The building looked like Seattle's Space Needle and sported a casino on the first floor and another on the second level of the tower. It was open, but it never made a profit. Like Howard's other casinos, it struggled from the start.

At Kerkorian's International, the huge showroom opened with Barbra Streisand and Elvis Presley. The Elvis show sold out for all 30 days of his contract, and the property was filled with happy gamblers. Next, Kerkorian's International Leisure company bought the Flamingo, before both the International and Flamingo were sold to Hilton Hotels.

Kerkorian's success in Las Vegas led to his purchase of the MGM movie studio, and the building of the MGM Grand Hotel. Spun-off from Metro-Goldwyn-Mayer, MGM Resorts was born. Today, MGM

Resorts is the largest casino company in the world. Some of its Las Vegas resorts include the Bellagio, MGM Grand, The Mirage, New York-New York, Circus-Circus, Excalibur, The Luxor, and Mandalay Bay.

As for Howard Hughes, after purchasing the Desert Inn, he kept right on buying properties he planned to upgrade and turn into winners. Virtually every casino he purchased had already reached its peak and was in decline, if not free-fall. His ego told him that by simply buying them, he could make them profitable. The list of casinos included Harold's Club in Reno, which was purchased in 1970 under the name "Summa Corporation." It is difficult to guess how well the city of Las Vegas would have done in the 1970s and '80's had it not been for Howard Hughes pumping–in some $300 million dollars to buy out and refurbish the struggling casinos around town.

He was well ahead of his time in putting up electronically secured surroundings and trying to offer visitors a "family" vacation, and Howard made "Middle America" believe that Las Vegas was acceptable. Soon, most of the casinos would be part of national corporations and listed on Wall Street. It spelled a new age for Las Vegas and Nevada as a whole.

Howard rarely slept, and he liked to see the old movies on TV at 2 am. When the local station started playing modern shows, Hughes tried to buy the station. It wasn't for sale. When repeated letters and phone calls didn't get the station to change back to old movies, he bought KLAS-TV and played the movies he wanted all night long.

However, even with the casinos, and the movies, Howard was still unhappy with Las Vegas. Mostly, it was the damn government blowing off all those nuclear bombs at the Nevada Test Site. He could feel the shock waves they produced all the way out on the Strip and up in his tenth-floor penthouse. He was also concerned about the potential risk of radiation poisoning to the air and water supply. He wrote memo after memo to Maheu and William Gay to send to his Nevada representatives in Congress, and when that didn't work, he told Maheu to offer President Nixon a $1 million bribe. Strangely, that didn't work.

The casino buying stopped, the nuclear tests continued, and

Howard slipped out of the Desert Inn one night and made his way to the Bahamas. His impact on Las Vegas lasted for years.

16 OTHER PEOPLE'S MONEY

Jimmy Hoffa is rarely credited with anything ever done in Las Vegas, whereas Bugsy Siegel is often considered the mastermind behind the whole city, even though his time in Sin City lasted only a few years and resulted in a grotesquely expensive hotel that cost him his life due to its excessive cost. Too bad Bugsy didn't know Hoffa, they might both have lived longer!

The Mob hated spending their money on anything but the essentials, like bribes and political kickbacks. The idea of spending capital to build casinos was a foreign idea, one they loathed. Look how cranky they got when Bugsy Siegel kept spending their hard-stolen bucks on the Flamingo! So, while some of the casinos in Kentucky, Ohio, and Arkansas were very nice, they weren't built from the ground up.

After the Flamingo, the Desert Inn was the first quality property built without outside investor money and building it with his own cash almost killed Moe Dalitz, but he made Las Vegas his home, and he wanted to improve the community. So, he set his mind to finding a way to make changes with other people's money, and who had a lot of money? Why the Teamsters union, of course!

After Moe Dalitz had watched Jimmy Hoffa betray his union brothers for $25,000, they stayed on speaking terms. Both men knew the other was powerful, and powerful friends are the best to stay in touch with. You just never know when such a friendship might be valuable again someday.

Someday arrived in 1959 when Moe and his Desert Inn partners decided to build a hospital for the community, their community. The 100-bed Sunrise Hospital went through a long chain of businesses names and holding accounts, but the result was a $1 million dollar loan from the Teamsters Central States, Southeast, and Southwest Areas Pension Fund. Hoffa signed as one of the beneficiaries. When it was done, or nearly done, the hospital was permitted to open with a dozen building code violations and fourteen plumbing violations, but hey, it was just a hospital.

To make sure it was a good deal for everyone involved, Dalitz and Hoffa arranged for the hospital to keep five beds available for the basic medical care of the Teamsters and Culinary Workers union employees, at the cost of just $6.50 per union member per month. How many union workers were there in Vegas at the time? A lot. In fact, by 1963 there were nearly 8,000. So over $50,000 was coming in monthly! The paperwork and loan went through quickly, mostly because Teamster officials did not have to account for expenditures of pension funds that they loaned out, even to themselves.

Once the new funding source was proven, it was put to serious use. The next beneficiaries were the Fremont Hotel owners, who got $850,000 in 1961 as part of their package of loans for expansion. The cool part was that the deal was assigned to Three-O-One Corporation. The president was Icepick Alderman, and the vice president was Allard Roen. The loan went through even though three days earlier; Roen was indicted in New York court on a stock-fraud charge in the United Dye and Chemical case. He later pleaded guilty to securities fraud.

Of course, by the time the Fremont Hotel had all their loans wrapped together they got a total of $4 million from the Teamsters fund. Major Riddle, who owned nearly 40 percent of the Dunes by the late 1950s, got a similar amount, and Dalitz and Roen picked up a little over $1 million to build the Stardust Golf Course.

Things didn't end too well for Jimmy Hoffa. He was indicted on charges of fraudulently obtaining $20 million in loans from the Teamsters Pension Fund and taking $1.2 million of the loan for himself and his co-conspirators. He received a five-year prison sentence. He was head of the Teamsters Union at the time.

Later, in 1964, he was convicted of bribery and tampering with a grand jury. That sentence was for 13 years. He had served a total of 58 months before President Richard Nixon commuted his sentence to time served. He was happy being sprung from jail but unhappy that Nixon had added a stipulation that Hoffa could have nothing to do with the union until 1980, but Hoffa didn't live that long.

In an interesting turn of events, three important men connected to the casinos of Las Vegas and the Mob died in 1975. At the time, the Church Committee of the US Senate was investigating intelligence activities of the FBI and CIA, including information gathered before and after the assassination of JFK, and the opening of mail of US citizens by the intelligence community.

The Church Committee learned that over a 20-year period, the CIA and FBI intercepted, opened and photographed more than 215,000 pieces of mail. The program, called "HTLINGUAL," was shut down in 1973. However, FBI notes from the 1940s show agents given the go-ahead to intercept the mail of certain persons of interest, including Bugsy Siegel.

As for the investigation of a plot by the CIA to use the Mob to kill Castro and possible backlash that may have led to the killing of JFK, or even the Mob's role in the assassination, over 50,000 pages of documents have been declassified, but not all of them. What could be so important about documents from the 1960s and 1970s? Perhaps something about the death of three individuals all scheduled to appear before the Committee.

Sam Giancana joined the FBI witness program and had police protection. On June 19, 1975, his police protection was called off. Giancana had a heart condition and couldn't eat spicy foods, but was frying sausage and peppers at his stove, perhaps for a friend who had come to dine. That was the exact moment when a gunman shot him in the back of the head. He pitched forward onto the stove, spilling hot grease and sausages across the kitchen floor, and then fell to the ground. The shooter rolled him over and pumped six more shots into his head and neck. He never testified.

Johnny Roselli did testify before the Committee on June 24, 1975. His testimony included his involvement in Operation Mongoose, the CIA plot to kill Castro. Shortly after Giancana's murder, Roselli moved from Los Angeles to Miami, Florida.

Jimmy Hoffa disappeared on July 30, 1975, from the parking lot of the Machus Red Fox Restaurant outside of Detroit. His disappearance is still a mystery to this day. He never testified.

Roselli was recalled by the committee to testify about the conspiracy to kill President Kennedy, but he disappeared. On August 9, 1976, his body washed up in a southern bay inside a 55-gallon steel drum. He had been stabbed and strangled. His legs were cut off to accommodate the size of the drum.

As for the Teamster's Pension Fund, money flowed to most any property that had the need, and the connections. Up in Reno, Mert Wertheimer sold his Riverside Hotel casino to a group of businessmen from Detroit (yes, he was originally from Detroit too) and they received nearly $2 million in Teamster funds to refurbish the tired, old facility. It didn't help business much. In fact, the casino was doing so poorly that the bosses started switching in loaded dice when the need arose on the craps games. They were caught and pleaded ignorance of any improprieties. The property was closed shortly after that in 1967.

At the Silver Slipper, the same defense was used for their dice cheating scandal. The club was closed on the spot when crooked dice were found on one of the craps games. The owners claimed ignorance but floated the possibility that they had been planted there by an employee. Well, of course, they were put there by an employee, geez.

It was an employee that was caught cheating two months later, too, when a blackjack dealer was repeatedly seen dealing "seconds," and this time the Gaming Commission shut the casino down for good, license gone.

That wasn't the case with the Tallyho Motel, which opened without gaming in 1962. It closed in 1963 without any scandals. Two months later it was the King's Crown, but its owners couldn't get a gaming license either. The next year Milton Prell bought the little resort and opened the Aladdin. It didn't make any money.

In 1969 Parvin Dohrman Corp. bought the casino and sold it to Sam Diamond, Richard Daly, St. Louis politician Peter Webbe, and well-known mob attorney Sorkis Webbe. The hotel was upgraded at the cost of $60 million, which included a 19-story tower and a 7,500-seat indoor arena. The property struggled financially while those around it prospered. What gives?

In August 1979, four men were convicted by a federal grand jury in Detroit for conspiring to allow hidden owners to exert control over the Aladdin, prompting the Nevada Gaming Commission to close the hotel. U.S. District Judge Harry Claiborne stated that he had "special powers" as a federal judge out to protect the interests of Nevada. And, he had allowed the property to reopen (Claiborne was indicted by a federal grand jury for bribery, fraud, and tax evasion charges in December 1983 and was impeached by the United States House of Representatives on July 22, 1986).

In September of 1979, the Aladdin Hotel Corp., Sorkis Webbe (yeah, that's a person), and Del Webb Corp. were indicted on charges of conspiracy to defraud the Teamsters Union during the 1975-76 Aladdin remodeling. The indictment alleged that subcontractors were forced to pay kickbacks during construction totaling $2.5 million. Del Webb Corp. at the time owned the Sahara Tahoe, Sahara Reno, and the Sahara Las Vegas. The casinos changed hands quickly afterward.

The following year, entertainer Wayne Newton purchased the Aladdin casino. It had trouble making payroll and struggled for two years until Newton sold out. In 1984 the property went into bankruptcy. It had repeated the trick in 1988 and 1997 before it was imploded in 1998, but like Dracula, it came back from the dead and reopened with the same name in 2000. Of course, nothing had changed, even with a new building. It had the same financial troubles and was sold in bankruptcy in 2003. It is now Planet Hollywood.

Las Vegas casino owners have often been seen as having too much money, and occasionally the wrong people get the wrong idea about how to get some of it. Dealer theft of chips is common, so is a little embezzlement, and those problems are always dealt with quickly. So are problems that require a little more muscle.

With all the money in Vegas, casino owners weren't immune from plots against them. According to police, in 1967, cab driver Marvin Shumate and a buddy dreamed up a plot to kidnap Benny Binion's younger son, Teddy, who was a friend of Shumate's son. They figured it would be easy to snatch Teddy, hold him for $100,000 in ransom money, and then turn him loose. Shumate's fellow cab driver was fine with the idea until the plan was changed to kill Teddy to keep him from being a witness.

Unfortunately for Shumate, his buddy got cold feet and went to Benny and spilled the whole plot. He was allowed to leave town, alive. Shumate wasn't so lucky. Tom Hanley and his son, Gramby, took Shumate up to Sunrise Mountain and blew half his face away with a shotgun blast and a few stray bullets from a .38 revolver.

After the body was found, evidence pointed to the Hanley's, so Alphonse Bass, a friend, and bodyguard were picked up for questioning. He intimated that the Hanley's might have been involved, but he was never able to testify. His body was found in a torched house, tied to a chair.

Tom Hanley was suspected in several other murders, including the killing of union agent James Hartley, found shot in the head and dumped in the desert. Hanley also was a suspect in several bombings, including a dynamite blast in 1972.

William Coulthard ran the Las Vegas FBI office from 1939 to 1945. He married Lena Silvagni, daughter of P.O. Silvagni, who built and owned the Apache Hotel, the first air-conditioned hotel in Las Vegas. When Lena passed away in 1955, she left her husband her share of the Apache land, 37 percent of the property where Binion's Horseshoe stood.

Coulthard was involved in lease negotiations with Benny Binion, where the land lease hadn't had an increase in 10 years. The negotiations were later described as "heated," as Binion accused Coulthard of trying to "Jack up the rent to improve your casino," because Coulthard was a corporate officer and stockholder of the Four Queens casino across the street.

On July 25, 1972, Coulthard went to his parked Cadillac on the 3rd floor of the parking terrace adjacent to his office in the Bank of Nevada building. He climbed into the car and turned the ignition, which tripped a clothespin trigger that ignited three sticks of dynamite planted beneath the engine near the steering column.

The resulting explosion demolished the Cadillac, and fire spread to five other vehicles. Another 20 cars were damaged. The force of the blast blew a hole in the concrete floor of the parking garage down to the second floor and shattered light fixtures in the Bank of Nevada. Coulthard's body was so badly charred that the only way for investigators to confirm his identity was through his dental charts.

In 1976, Culinary Union boss Al Bramlet contracted with Tom and Gramby Hanley to help him convince local restaurants that they should be union shops. Some resisted. Bramlet told Hanley to bomb the restaurants, and one was. Two others, the Village Pub and Starboard Tack, were targeted, but the car bombs there were duds, and neither exploded.

According to later court testimony, the Hanley's wanted to be paid for all three bombs, but Bramlet refused to pay for the two that did not ignite, only the one at David's Place on West Charleston, where the bomb exploded. When Bramlet returned from a trip to Reno on February 24, 1977, he was in for an ugly surprise when the Hanley's and Eugene Vaughan met him at McCarran Airport.

They cornered him when he exited the plane and forced him to the parking lot where they had a van waiting. Tom gave him a quick punch to the side of the head, knocking him down. As his eye swelled, Bramlet's wrists were handcuffed behind his back. "All we want is to get paid; you don't want to die for ten-grand, do you?" Tom asked. Bramlet said "No, I'll get the cash," so the group stopped at a pay phone, and Bramlet called Syd Wyman at the Dunes Hotel and told him he needed $10,000 for a personal matter. "Take it to Benny Binion down at the Horseshoe," Bramlet said. Wyman agreed.

Bramlet was then gagged and driven into the nearby desert where he was repeatedly shot and dumped in a shallow grave. The case unraveled quickly after that, and the Hanley's were put on trial for murder as well as attempted murder for the car bombings. They were both sentenced to life in prison without parole. Tom Hanley lasted only months in prison before he died of what were called natural causes.

17 WHO'S MAKING MONEY?

Now we know that not every casino in Las Vegas made money, Mob-owned or not. Even clubs on the Strip like the Royal Nevada closed because they were too small, or too poorly run to pay the bills. Others, like the Castaway's and Silver Slipper casinos, struggled for years, managing to stay just ahead of the tax collector. At the Hacienda Casino, Doc Bayley ran the resort at near break-even until he passed away in 1964 and then Judy Bayley ran the club until 1971 when she passed away. Of course, "ran the club," is a relative term.

The following year, Paul W. Lowden purchased 15% of the Hacienda with some partners and made himself the entertainment director. One of the partners brought in Allen Glick, a young, land developer from San Diego who purchased controlling interest. The Hacienda was reasonably priced because it had always struggled, unlike the Tropicana, which make good money for the Mob for two decades.

In the 1950s, Frank Costello felt confident in making more Las Vegas investments after the success of the Flamingo and the Riviera., but he still wasn't willing to put much money into them. His slot machine partner in New Orleans, Phil Kastel, and the *don* of New Orleans, Carlos Marcello, had a contact at the Fontainebleau Hotel in Florida by the name of Ben Jaffe, and he was the perfect front for a new Vegas casino.

Kastel offered some cash (less than half-a-million), and a good construction company that had just finished the Riviera, the Taylor Construction Company of Miami, to Jaffe, and he fell right into the quicksand of the desert that had swallowed Ben Siegel ten years earlier.

The construction of the Tropicana started well enough, but as the building and its costs kept rising, Ben Jaffe was forced to sell his interest in the Fontainebleau for $3 million. He was beside himself; he loved the property. How had he gotten himself mixed up in the desert of Las Vegas he wondered? Next came another $3 million from his insurance company holdings. By the time the club was ready to open on April 4, 1957, the total investment was $10 million, much of it from Ben Jaffe. Louis Lederer and J. Kell Houssels, Sr. were licensed to run the South Beach Miami – themed casino.

After Costello had got caught with the casino's gross gaming numbers in his pocket, Louis Lederer, who's handwriting was detected on the slip in Costello's pocket, was forced to sell his interest in the Tropicana. This, of course, would make everything fine and no hoodlums would be involved in running the club, right? The Gaming Control Board was delusional again, but it looked good in the press.

So did the Tropicana's winnings, when it was announced it was the highest earning casino in Las Vegas, and that was after the standard skim. According to the records of the Gaming Control Board, Harold's Club in Reno and Harrah's Club at South Shore

Lake Tahoe were the biggest-earning casinos in the state at the time. When Bill Harrah purchased George's Gateway Club at Lake Tahoe in 1955, he remarked, "We were doing great in Reno, and here was this tiny club in Tahoe doing twice what we were."

However, to believe that a beautiful new hotel-casino in Las Vegas could be out-earned by a seasonal property in the Sierra Nevada Mountains that had no hotel was ridiculous. The skim in Las Vegas was enormous, and casinos like the Fremont, Stardust, Desert Inn, Riviera, Sands, Dunes, and Flamingo provided most of it. The Tropicana, right there with the best, continued to grow and provide a steady income for their owners, and even a little for their front men.

The FBI estimates that at the height of the Mob's control, their casinos were being skimmed for over a million dollars each day. The casinos were run in a manner that was strong enough to pay for everything else on the property. The restaurants, showroom, hotel rooms, and other guest facilities did not have to make money. When there were less than 1,000 rooms and a few restaurants and bars, the cost of the rooms and meals were kept at bargain rates.

Visitors to Las Vegas in the 1950s through the 1970s expected to get a great steak dinner for ten bucks, and a nice room for $29.95 and you know what? The properties never suffered. They were casinos with hotel rooms. A vacation was a bargain, even if you dropped a few hundred in the slots, so what? There was a pool for the kids, mom and dad could party a little, and everyone went home happy.

Unhappy with today's Las Vegas prices? Blame the men who thought the resorts needed to have 98 percent of the space occupied by shops, restaurants, bars, and hotel rooms. When you've got 5,000 rooms, they've got to provide a pretty good revenue stream – especially when the casino only occupies 2 percent of the floor space! So, that's progress. And not every casino could make it.

Casinos changed hands, new deals between crime families were common, and new front-men were brought in on a revolving door basis throughout the 1960s. Once Howard Hughes's properties were shored-up internally, there were fewer Mob-controlled casinos. Still, there was plenty of money to go around.

After Paul W. Lowden got into the Hacienda in 1971, he found out he could also buy into the Tropicana. He purchased a $500,000 stake in the casino but began to worry about his partners and the control of Mafia figure Joseph Agosto. The man Lowden had brought in, Alan Glick, had no such worries. In 1976, Lowden asked the Tropicana's Board of Directors to repurchase his share in the property. They refused. Lowden was so shaken by his predicament he walked away from his $500,000 investment at the Trop.

As it turned out, Lowden got the last laugh when Agosto and his boys were forced to relinquish their licenses to the Nevada Gaming Control Board. Lowden got his stake in the casino back, just in time to see his partner from the Hacienda start a fall from grace with the state, and the Mob.

Agosto first slipped into the Tropicana as the manager of the "Folies Bergere" show and was an employee of the production company. In April 1975, Agosto was arrested by U.S. Immigration Services as an illegal immigrant, but attorney Oscar Goodman beat the immigration charge, and Agosto went back to work at the Tropicana for owners Ed and Fred Doumani. Unfortunately, before he got the skim set up, Mitzi Stauffer Briggs purchased 51 percent of the Tropicana's stock. She was new to the casino, but went on instinct, keeping Briggs at arm's length. Eventually, he gained her trust, so he broke it.

The skim finally started for the Kansas City family in 1977. By then the property was more profitable, and a little extra could be safely taken off the top each day. On Valentine 's Day, 1979, the FBI used their electronic and visual surveillance to capture a courier with $80,000 in skim. It only took them 11 months, unless you count the other 22 years the property was known to be skimming.

Both Nick Civella and Agosto were indicted, along with eight other defendants. Nick Civella died in 1983. Agosto turned informant, as so many other cornered rats have, and became the government's star witness. Carl Civella, Nick's son, got 35 years.

One property that always made money was Caesars Palace, and if any casino in the 1960s stood out as the epitome of Las Vegas, it was Caesars Palace. Jay Sarno and Stanley Mallin opened the perfect high-roller property in 1964, using Teamster Pension funds to finance the $24 million venture. Some friends helped them run the casino.

During the Second World War, Sarno and Mallin ran crap games, finding unsophisticated soldiers who were happy to play a game with bad odds and high rates for cash loans after they lost their pay. When they got home, the partners tried several businesses together, but keeping a crap game going helped make ends meet.

When they ran short of cash, the partners moved to Atlanta Georgia where they worked in bars, did some contract construction work, and rolled the bones. After a few good scores, they bought a dilapidated building and started construction on a series of motor lodges. Sarno hired Jo Harris, a young interior designer, and they began comparing notes on how to use lighting, mirrors, and exterior fountains to enhance the property's appeal. That foundation would someday be Sarno's gift to Vegas.

As their designs took shape, the money arrived to build the Atlanta Cabana Motel after Jimmy Hoffa, and Allen Dorfman arranged a $1.8 million loan from the Teamsters Union Central States Pension Fund. Hoffa's cut for his "help" was a modest $36,000. The motel opened in 1958.

Hoffa, always ready to line his pockets, arranged a second loan for twice the amount so that Sarno could build the Dallas Cabana the following year. During construction, Sarno spent his free time up in Las Vegas. He liked playing craps more than building motels, and after building a third property using Roman architecture in Palo Alto, California in 1962, he was convinced he should build in Las Vegas. By then, he had lost over $500,000 at the Desert Inn and Riviera casinos, all in cash.

Vegas had all the trappings of ancient Rome, gold, wine, women, and Sarno took advantage of everything offered by the casinos for his pleasure. What the casinos didn't have was class. They were cheap, nothing more than a facade. Sarno wanted to offer more. Wine, women, and song, but with class.

Later that year, Sarno signed a lease for a plot of land owned by Kirk Kerkorian, north of Flamingo Road. Hoffa and Dorfman signed as beneficiaries of a new $20 million loan to build Caesar's Palace, and Sarno based the design of the property on ancient Rome. Built to cater to each customer as though they were Roman emperors, the Bacchanal Room restaurant even offered waitresses dressed in Roman togas who poured wine for the diners and massaged their shoulders.

The new property was an immediate success, and high-rollers flocked to the property. Although expected to fail by old-time Vegas pundits, the property was a virtual news-maker from the day it opened with beautiful girls wandering the property, white Roman columns, and water fountains large enough to jump a motorcycle over, which is exactly what Evil Knievel did in 1967. Well, kind of. Although his 141-foot motorcycle jump over the fountain was successful, his landing was not.

Knievel was said to be in a coma for 29 days with a crushed pelvis and femur, fractures to his hip, wrist and both ankles, and he missed the greatest media frenzy Caesars, and Las Vegas had ever experienced. Sports Illustrated and ABC-TV's Wide World of Sports did extensive stories about Knievel, the failed jump, and Caesars Palace. Across the country, hundreds of other media outlets featured stories about Las Vegas, where gambling of all kinds was obviously accepted.

The casino made more money than Sarno ever dreamed it would. In fact, it was so successful that money was funneled to secret owners for five years before the U.S. government started investigating the Teamster loans and some questionable financial moves by the casino managers. But that wasn't a problem; the Mob did what it always did, it brought in a new front.

This time, it was Stuart and Clifford Perlman, who started their business venture as Lums Inc. with a hot dog stand in Miami Beach in 1956. They were very successful, and by 1965 the brother's controlled 15 restaurants. They also had a friend in Miami named Meyer Lansky. Lansky, as always, had a hidden interest in the company and benefited from the casino win at Caesars after the Perlman's bought the property from Sarno for $58 million. They also changed their business name to Caesars World.

Caesars continued to make tons of money, and in 1972, Caesars World bought the Thunderbird Casino, from Del Webb Corporation for $13.6 million. The plan was to turn the old property into a gleaming new resort called the Mark Anthony, continuing the Roman theme of Caesars. Strangely enough, Caesars World was unable to find financing for the planned $150-million, 2,000-room resort. In

1976 they dumped the non-producing property for $9 million, using the money to start construction in Atlantic City.

There, Caesars purchased the old Howard Johnson's hotel and built the $70 million Caesars Boardwalk Regency, which opened in 1979. Unfortunately for the Perlman's, their association with Meyer Lansky did not go unnoticed by the Atlantic City regulators or those in Nevada. The brothers were forced to sell their holdings in Caesars World for $98 million in 1980.

Sarno, of course, went on to build Circus-Circus, which he sold in 1974. His love for Las Vegas and Caesars Palace never ended. Known to lose $100,000 in an evening of craps, Sarno died of a heart attack on July 21, 1984, while staying at his old casino, Caesars Palace.

18 LEFTY'S CURVEBALL

As the 1970s dawned on Las Vegas, several casinos like the Flamingo, Sands, Dunes, Tropicana, and the Riviera were showing their age. Every one of them was controlled by the Mob. Even after all the years of substantial income, the Mob hated to spend actual cash on building and renovation. The Tropicana, which had the highest grossing casino in Las Vegas for several years, was reduced to moderate to poorly reported income due to substantial skimming and a lack of reinvestment. The more it made, the higher the skim got, and the higher the wages got for Mob guys entrusted with keeping watch over the casinos.

Frank "Lefty" Rosenthal (born June 12, 1929) is remembered as one of the greatest bookies of all time, and one of the most crooked. He learned to set odds, game lines and ran the biggest illegal bookmaking office in the U.S. out of a company called Cicero Home Improvement. When he had the opportunity, he bribed players to throw games, boxing matches, and shave points, so the point spread was just right for the Chicago Outfit to win big.

When Sonny Liston fought Floyd Patterson, the fight odds on Liston had to go high enough to get more bets on Patterson. Strangely enough, Patterson's manager, Cus D'Amato, had his New York State license revoked over his underworld connections. The fight was held at Comiskey Park in Chicago, and bookmakers made plenty of money when Liston easily knocked out the heavyweight champion of the world.

Rosenthal moved to Miami, Florida and continued his work as a premier bookmaker. He was subpoenaed to appear before a Senate subcommittee on Gambling and Organized Crime, accused of match fixing. He pleaded the Fifth Amendment 37 times. The charges were dropped.

In 1964, Sonny Liston fought Cassius Clay in Miami. Rosenthal was at ringside. According to FBI documents (you know, the guys who see everything, but don't tell anyone until years later) Mob guys, Frankie Carbo and Blinky Palermo secretly owned Sonny Liston's contract. Liston was a 7-1 favorite but had to quit during the fight because of a sore shoulder. In the rematch, Listen was knocked-out by what became known as the "Phantom Punch," and Listen's loss, once again, won guys in-the-know a bundle of cash. Rosenthal knew everything that was coming.

Lefty was only convicted once, after pleading no contest to allegedly bribing New York University player Ray Paprocky to shave points for a college basketball game. The FBI compiled hundreds of pages of documents on Rosenthal, but he went to Las Vegas as a good citizen in 1968.

His income from Mob activities was modest until he had a hand in the Stardust, then he purchased a home at 972 Vegas Valley Drive. The house had a pool, 3,200 square feet of living space, and overlooked the golf course.

With Marshall Caifano and Johnny Roselli gone from the Las Vegas scene, Tony Accardo chose 32-year old Anthony Spilotro, who had already spent several years working with Rosenthal, as the new Las Vegas enforcer. FBI records show Spilotro was arrested 13 times in the 1950s for petty thefts like shoplifting and stealing purses. By the time FBI Special Agent Bill Roemer was following him around, it wasn't because he was stealing hubcaps.

The incident that sticks in most people's minds is how he handled Billy McCarthy after it was discovered he and a partner had killed two of Spilotro's gang members. Spilotro caught Billy in a South Side bar and took him to a local garage at gunpoint. Then he stabbed him in the groin repeatedly with an ice pick and jammed his head into a vice and slowly twisted the handle. After the man's left eye popped out, he finally gave up his partner. Then Spilotro killed him. Later he killed his partner. If the scene sounds familiar, it was recreated in the movie *Casino*, based on the Stardust casino, Lefty Rosenthal, and Tony Spilotro.

Spilotro was indicted, and Roemer described him as "That little piss ant," to the press. They changed the description to Tony "The Ant" Spilotro, but he didn't get time in the joint.

Tony went from the streets of Chicago to Miami Beach, Florida, before being given the Las Vegas job, at which point he packed with his wife, Nancy, and their son, Vincent, and moved there in 1971. He wasn't too wild with his living spaces, buying a modest, 2,400 square foot, one-story home at 4675 Balfour Drive near McLeod Drive and Tropicana Avenue.

The Ant got a stipend from the Mob's casinos, and he also got a new job: gift shop owner. Jay Sarno, who built Caesars Palace for the world's high-rollers, also built Circus Circus casino for players on the other end of the spectrum, but it wasn't doing too well on the Strip without any hotel rooms. So, Sarno and partner Stanley Mallin took a $23 million loan from the Teamsters Pension Fund to construct a hotel, and Tony Stuart (aka Tony Spilotro) got to run the gift shop. He was supposed to be licensed, but Sarno looked the other way. He was supposed to put up $70,000, but a loan was arranged.

Gift shops in Las Vegas are like little money factories. Players who win big in the casino like to buy gifts for loved-ones back home. So do players who lose so that they can take a peace-offering home with them. Most of the jewelry and knick-knacks in the gift shops have a huge markup of at least 800 percent. Spilotro did well with his gift shop, and even better when he sold it to the new owners of the casino in 1974 for $700,000.

During his time in Vegas, The Ant was indicted three times for murder. He beat the rap every time. His lawyer, Oscar Goodman, would go on to become mayor of Las Vegas twenty years later. It figures he must have been a hell of a lawyer!

Spilotro was also indicted by a federal grand jury in Chicago for defrauding the Central State Teamsters Pension Fund of $1.4 million. A co-defendant was Allen Dorfman, who was also a co-defendant with Jimmy Hoffa in the 1963 Jury-tampering case that sent Hoffa to prison. Dorfman took control of the Central States Pension Fund after Hoffa went to prison, and one of the loans he approved was for Stardust/Argent Corp.

Joseph Lombardo and Bugsy's old Las Vegas attorney Irwin Weiner were also indicted in 1974, for the $1.4 million loan to a bogus plastics manufacturing company in Deming, New Mexico. Everyone walked when informant Daniel Seifert was found murdered in September of 1974.

In 1979, the FBI launched Operation Pendorf (Penetration of Allen Dorfman) and bugged his Insurance Agency. Information obtained from the microphones led to an indictment of Dorman and four others in 1981. He was subsequently convicted in December 1982 with Teamsters' President Roy Lee Williams and Joseph Lombardo of conspiring to bribe Nevada Senator Howard Cannon. Dorfman was murdered in a Hyatt Hotel parking lot in Lincolnwood, Illinois, while walking with Irwin Weiner, possibly to keep him from cooperating with the FBI to avoid a 55-year prison sentence. Weiner was not injured, but could not accurately describe the assailant.

On June 23, 1973, William "Red" Klim was murdered in the parking lot of the Churchill Downs Race Book in Las Vegas. Spilotro was suspected. The crime was never solved.

While Spilotro ran wild in Las Vegas, even manning a crew of burglars called the "Hole in the Wall Gang," the Chicago family (as well as those in Milwaukee, St. Louis, and Kansas City) stayed mum while their casinos continued to skim enormous amounts of money.

With a little piece of the Hacienda and the Tropicana, young Allen Glick figured he had found the golden goose and was scouting around for another casino to invest in. Now he was interested in the Stardust and got into a conversation with Marty Buccieri, a pit boss at Caesars Palace. Buccieri told Glick he could help with a loan connection and the next thing Glick knew he was talking to a fellow named Frank Balistrieri, who promised to put in a good word with the Teamsters Central States Pension Fund. In short order, Glick owned the Stardust casino. He also owed nearly $140 million but was happy as a clam with his new Argent Corporation.

More meetings brought the Fremont and Marina casinos into his control, and the 29-year old was being called "The Golden Boy of Gaming," by the local newspapers, but there were clouds on the horizon.

After the purchase of the Stardust, Glick was summoned to Kansas City, Missouri, where he met with Nick Civella. Nick explained there was a $1.2 million fee for the family's assistance in getting his first $23 million Teamsters Central States Pension Fund loan. He was also told that Frank Rosenthal would be his director at the Stardust and that whatever Lefty said was the law of God. Glick gave a shaky smile and returned to Las Vegas.

Getting Lefty licensed wasn't as easy as getting Nick Civella paid. The Gaming Control Board rejected Rosenthal for the position of General Manager and then rejected him as the Poker room coordinator. After that, they rejected him as the assistant entertainment director too, but not until after he oversaw the construction of the new showroom that included several dozen tables not on the floor plans or the books so that the price of the tickets for those seats could go directly into his pocket.

He also orchestrated several other colorful ideas, such as the "scales skim." In the early '70's, the Stardust had 2000 slot machines. $1 slots were very popular, and because of the huge number of $1 tokens in use, coins were weighed in bags, instead of being counted. Then, the scales in the "hard count" room where all the buckets of coins were taken each morning at 4:00 am were rigged. Instead of each bag containing 500-dollar tokens, each bag had 510. And, to make sure the most could be made from the new scam, the hard count room at the Stardust was used for quarters and dollar tokens from the Fremont, Marina, and the Hacienda. It all looked like cost-cutting measures, using one facility, but it was all done to get more money to the Mob.

The scheme only had one problem. What to do with thousands of extra $1 tokens each night. Lefty Rosenthal to the rescue! He just had the casino's slot personnel buy them. Like the extra seats in the showroom, Lefty had two extra coin cabinets installed up on the casino floor that wasn't strictly kosher. Then, the bags delivered from hard count were opened, and the $1 tokens were put into racks of 100. The employees never knew what was going on. A boss would sign-in 100 bags totaling $50,000 and later, would sign out $50,000 in cash, which was taken to the soft count room. Another fellow came by and picked up the extra $1,000 in cash that had been produced.

Over the course of several years, the skim amounted to over $5 million. Pretty good for a few extra dollars a bag and never suspecting slot personnel on the payroll is doing all the work for you!

In 1975, Marty Buccieri, the Caesar's Palace pit boss, dropped by Glick's office and reminded him what he had done for him. "Where's the love, Allan, where's my end? I deserve at least a $30,000 finder's fee for getting you those huge loans from the Teamsters, right?"

Glick went to Rosenthal; Rosenthal went to Spilotro. Marty Buccieri was killed in Caesars' parking lot. Spilotro was suspected, but local officers couldn't come up with a motive. The crime was never solved.

Tamara Rand, a friend and business partner of Allen Glick's in San Diego who invested $2 million in his Vegas casinos, was hired as a consultant at the Hacienda. She asked what her 5% of the Hacienda was going to get her, now that the property was profitable. Glick denied he owed her anything for her investment. She was killed in San Diego. Spilotro and Glick both professed their innocence. The crime was never solved.

Meanwhile, the four casinos under Glick's name and the Mob's control, skimmed millions and millions of dollars while making very little for Glick. He was relegated to overseeing departments that were never intended to make a profit, like housekeeping.

It wasn't until June of 1978 that the Nevada Gaming Commission told Rosenthal that his duties, regardless of his job title, required him to obtain a gaming license. During the hearing, Chairman Harry Reid took offense to the verbally abusive Rosenthal. Lefty was refused any license at the Stardust.

Harry Reid didn't make too many friends as head of the Gaming

Control Board. One evening his wife checked under the hood of their car because the engine had been running rough for several days. When Landra Reid popped the hood, she was amazed to find an unexploded bomb. Lady Luck!

The Gaming Control Board also had questions about what was going on at the Tropicana, so to rid the property of its Mob connections, gaming regulators forced the casino to be sold to Ramada Corp. in 1979.

Meanwhile, Paul Lowden raised $21 million through Valley Bank and the First American National Bank of Nashville, Tennessee and bought out Glick and the other owners of the Hacienda. He then expanded the property and gave it a very fine $30 million facelift. The new convention center and 11-story 300-room tower helped the Hacienda compete with other expanding casino hotels in town.

Things weren't going so well for Spilotro by the close of the '70s, though. His income from the Stardust, Fremont, and Marina had dwindled to nearly nothing, and in 1979, an FBI raid on Gold Rush Ltd. at 228 W. Sahara Avenue produced $200,000 worth of stolen jewelry and gems. Spilotro, his brother Jon, Herbert Blitzstein, and Joseph Blasko, a recently fired Metro Police detective, were arrested.

As usual, the FBI had trouble with the court system. A judge later dismissed the racketeering case, stating that FBI agents had overstepped their authority.

As for Las Vegas car bombings, Bugsy's admonition that "We only kill our own," seemed weak in the face of many other bombings, mostly with dynamite, and it wasn't just Las Vegas that was seeing an increase in car bombs.

In Phoenix, *Arizona Republic* reporter Don Bolles wrote a series of stories documenting Arizona Racing Commission member Kemper Marley and his ties to the race track concessionaire company, Emprise. They highlighted the federal investigation of Emprise, located in Buffalo, New York and their association with prominent organized crime figures. The company was convicted and fined $10,000 in U.S. District Court in Los Angeles for its hidden ownership in the Frontier casino in Las Vegas.

On June 2, 1976, Bolles started his car in a Phoenix hotel parking lot, and a bomb exploded, mortally wounding him. He did mutter several words before lapsing into unconsciousness, including "Adamson, Emprise, Mafia." After his death, John Harvey Adamson pleaded guilty to second-degree murder in 1977.

19 BEYOND THE MOB

In 1979, under pressure from the Gaming Control Board, Allen Glick's Argent Corp. was sold to Trans-Sterling Corp., which was heralded in the newspapers as a final death-blow to organized crime's control of the casinos in Nevada. For visitors to Las Vegas, the news was interesting, but not earth-shattering. So, the Mob was being pushed out of Nevada's casinos, yeah, whatever.

Of course, it wasn't as easy as all that. Not every mob guy just up and left town. There were plenty of Wise Guys still roaming the casinos and looking to make money. Las Vegas has a worldwide appeal. It's a 24-hour town where you won't be denied anything if you have the money. It doesn't matter if you're a gambler who gets lucky, a poker player who has the talent to win, or a Mob guy who loves the nightlife. Why leave?

If you don't believe that, look at the life of someone like Stu Unger, who showed more raw talent for no-limit poker than anyone did in the 1980s. He moved to Las Vegas, won the World Series of Poker twice, as well as several other tournaments, lost most of his money playing golf against the likes of Doyle Brunson, and betting sports, and was broke before the decade was out. His 24-hour lifestyle was legendary. He drank, he smoked, and he used cocaine like it was candy, which it was for him, just a little more expensive.

On the third day of 1990 WSOP main event Unger was the chip leader, but passed out in a hotel room on drugs and couldn't continue. His stacks were blinded-off, and he still finished 9th. He rallied, got semi-sober, and won the main event again for the third time in 1997 with the help of his friends. He died in 1998 in a cheap Vegas hotel room. He was 45 years old. That's just about how long the Mob lasted in Las Vegas, 45 years.

It joined the party late, stayed up all night for years, bled several casino properties dry, and just couldn't stay off the skim, the Mob's candy, long enough to do any real renovations and move into the 1980s. A few mobsters, most notably Moe Dalitz, were able to transition from a life devoted to crime, to one that gave up most of the hard stuff. Dalitz owned the Sundance Casino downtown after selling the Desert Inn to Howard Hughes. He devoted most of his time to playing golf but also contributed his time and money to local charities.

Dalitz teamed with friends Allard Roen, Mervyn Adelson, and Irwin Molasky in the 1970s to build the La Costa Resort in San Diego. Much of the financing was handled again by the Teamsters pension fund. *Penthouse* magazine ran an article in 1975 headlined *La Costa: The Hundred-Million-Dollar Resort with Criminal Clientele*. In response, the builders and owners sued the magazine for $522 million. The case went back and forth for years, and although a jury upheld Penthouse's right to print the article and found their reporting to be accurate, the case was thrown out by a judge.

In 1985, a state appellate court reinstated the 10-year-old libel case by Dalitz, Roen, and the others. At that time the two sides settled. No money changed hands, although the lawyers for both groups must have done quite well.

Records show that in 1975, the FBI was investigating loans (ten or twelve personal loans) made by United States National Bank, which handled the cash for Rancho La Costa through the Teamsters Pension Fund, made to Morris Barney Dalitz. According to the report, "loans were 'written off' at USNB as financial fees for Dalitz's influence to get the Central States Teamster Pension Fund to deposit millions of dollars with USNB at a time the bank badly needed the deposits."

The FBI report also states, "The Register of loans made by USNB for the years 1969 and 1970 was searched for loans obtained by the subject and no loans in the name of Moe Dalitz as borrower were found." However, directly below this statement, a list of loans written-off, but issued to another named individual, are listed. Unfortunately, the name of the recipient is redacted (crossed out).

As for other owners and casino properties, Howard Hughes purchased most of the previously Mob-controlled casinos in the 1960s. Several of them were closed over the years. The ones that stayed open were eventually sold to companies, instead of individual owners. Hughes also purchased Harold's Club in Reno, in 1970. He was impressed by the casino's ability to win so much money in Reno when compared with much larger properties in Las Vegas, but that too was a Las Vegas illusion.

By the time Hughes got his hands on the casino, it was in decline – as was Reno, and finally, the truth came out. Many of the larger properties in Vegas had been reporting much lower earnings due to the heavy skim of the profits. And that continued even into the 1980s.

When the Stardust owners were forced to sell their holdings to Trans-Sterling, Allan Sachs, and Herb Tobman were licensed to take over the casino on the Strip and also the Fremont casino in downtown Las Vegas, based on their "sterling character." Five years later, in 1984, Sachs and Tobman were fined $3 million dollars and had their licenses rescinded for failing to take "appropriate action" to prevent skimming from the two casinos. Like others before them, of course, they pleaded ignorance of any wrong-doing and said they didn't know all that cash was going to Kansas City. Whatever.

Sachs and Tobman had long careers in the gaming industry. Sachs worked his way up from a dealer position in illegal Chicago clubs, to pit boss in Cuban casinos. He opened the Royal Nevada in 1955 and held an interest in the Tropicana. In the 1970s he became president of the Stardust.

Tobman's gaming career started in the 1950s when he was general manager of the Moulin Rouge, which had serious financial problems. He had worked for two other clubs before he became the general manager of the Aladdin, which went into bankruptcy. Sachs was president of the Stardust in 1974 when he promoted Tobman to vice president. Long story short, they were both working or managing properties that had skim money going out the door. Perfect for the new owners of the Stardust and Fremont. Way to go Nevada Gaming Control Board! Both men professed their innocence of taking any skim or working with the Mob. In that case, for years and years, they were both grossly incompetent.

Frank Rosenthal was still in Vegas in the 1980s, hanging around the periphery of the casinos, and still fighting the Gaming Control Board over his exclusion from the Stardust. In 1982 he had dinner at Marie Calender's restaurant at 600 E. Sahara Avenue with three friends, Ruby Goldstein, Stanley Green, and Marty Kane. He then walked to his car, got in, and turned the key. The resulting explosion demolished his car.

The blast was so strong it blew the windows out of the back of the restaurant. Luckily for Lefty, a metal plate below the vehicle deflected much of the force of the bomb. Local ATF Special Agent John Rice said the high explosive went up, out and back toward the restaurant.

Rosenthal refused to sign a crime report and was transported to Sunrise Hospital, the same hospital the Teamsters money paid for with loans through Jimmy Hoffa. Lefty was released from the hospital several days later with nothing to show from the blast but some hearing damage and burns to his legs, left arm, and the left side of his face. He moved to Laguna Niguel, California shortly after that.

He was placed in Nevada's Black Book of undesirables in 1988, showing that the Gaming Control Board was on top of things.

Although the case was never solved, Milwaukee crime boss Frank Balistrieri had been heard on FBI wiretaps saying he blamed Lefty for the Mob's problems in Las Vegas and he "was going to get full satisfaction from him."

Balistrieri, sometimes called the "Mad Bomber," became Milwaukee's family boss in 1961. He was college educated but learned the business from his father-in-law, then crime boss, Joe Alioto. Balistrieri arranged the Teamster loans for Allen Glick and took the skim from the Stardust and Fremont for distribution to the families in Kansas City, Chicago, Milwaukee, and Cleveland.

In 1977, during an FBI sting operation, Special Agent Joseph Pistone, worked undercover in New York under the name Donnie Brasco (yeah, there's a movie called that). He then went to Milwaukee and set up a vending machine business to antagonize Balistrieri, trying to get him to make a move they could prosecute him for. When the men finally met, Balistrieri told him, "It's a good thing you came to see me and show me some respect. I was getting ready to kill you."

As for the Las Vegas skim, Balistrieri and Civella feuded over just how much each family should get. They were so antagonistic the only thing they could agree on was to go to arbitration presided by the Chicago Outfit. They both lost. Outfit leader Joseph Aiuppa and underboss John Cerone demanded that The Outfit receives an additional 25% from the cut Kansas City and Milwaukee were getting. Now that's funny.

In 1983, Balistrieri and his two sons were indicted on charges of skimming at the Stardust and Fremont casinos. Balistrieri was convicted on five charges. He received a sentence of 13 years in prison. His sons were convicted of extorting a local vending machine route operator and received two-year prison sentences.

Tony Spilotro wasn't so lucky. He and his brother Michael left for a meeting on June 14, 1986, two days before the start of the second "Hole in the Wall Gang" burglary and fencing trial in Las Vegas. They were never seen alive again, but their battered bodies were later found buried in an Indiana cornfield. Sand found in their lungs during an autopsy indicated they had been buried alive. Tony Spilotro was 48 years old at the time of his death.

A year later, Steve Wynn reinvented the Las Vegas Strip. He was making millions with his Golden Nugget Casinos and had a clear vision for what was to come. By then he had refurbished the downtown Las Vegas facility and also built the Atlantic City, New Jersey Golden Nugget Hotel & Casino. The New Jersey resort was a 1980 partnership of Golden Nugget Companies and Michael R. Milken worth $140 million. Milken was a wheeler-dealer and junk-bond king. His activities attracted the attention of the SEC, but not before he was able to raise $630 million dollars to fund the building of Wynn's Mirage.

The Mirage was considered extremely high-risk because Las Vegas was in a gaming slump characterized by older properties, smaller conventions, and a drop in gaming revenues. The new resort featured a South Sea's theme and an erupting volcano, and the property's high cost and emphases on luxury were cited as reasons the property would likely fail. Steve Wynn, of course, had the last laugh, as the property was enormously successful.

With the success of the Mirage, Wynn continued to expand on the Strip with Treasure Island and the Bellagio. Milken also helped obtain financing for Harrah's Entertainment, Mandalay Resorts, MGM, and Park Place. He fell from grace in 1989 when he was indicted for racketeering and securities fraud. He eventually pleaded guilty to securities and reporting violations and was sentenced to ten years in prison. He was also fined $600 million, (more than all the taxes the Mob saved with their skim of Las Vegas casinos) and permanently barred from the securities industry. His sentence was then reduced to just two years for good behavior, and cooperating with testimony against his former colleagues. The charges and prison term didn't stop his income, and at this time Mr. Milken is worth approximately $2.5 billion.

In the 1980s, the Nevada Gaming Control Board made some changes to their internal control policies for casinos. Minimum Internal Control procedures were implemented, and new audit directives came into being. Today, the Audit Division has a professional staff of 89 employees and is run like a CPA firm.

According to the NGCB, "The Audit Division is primarily responsible for auditing Group 1 casinos throughout the state (i.e., those casinos with annual gaming revenue of approximately $5.87 million or more). Presently, there are approximately 148 such casinos, and the audit cycle is about 2.3 years."

Also, audit personnel can request paperwork, view actual procedures of departments like the cage's "soft count," where the cash is counted, and review transaction logs. Skimming profits, as was often the norm in the days leading up to the 1980s, certainly wouldn't be an easy task today. Beyond the tax benefits to the state of the Board's new procedures, keeping the money visible and the owners accountable also tends to increase reinvestment in the state's gaming establishments.

It would appear that the Mob has been evicted from Las Vegas, but the legend of bosses like Gus Greenbaum, Moe Dalitz, and Bugsy Siegel will live forever. It's a testament to the expansion and mystique they created in a desert of sand few ever wanted to visit, much less own, before they arrived and changed the way the world saw Las Vegas.

Meyer Lansky, financially strained by his losses in Cuba in 1960, continued to live quietly in Miami Beach, Florida. He organized the skim disbursement from Las Vegas casinos for several crime families and dabbled in real estate and casino ownership, all under the table, until the end of his life. He died of lung cancer on January 15, 1983, age 80.

Although the FBI estimated that he accumulated over $300 million before he died, it is likely that most of the money he controlled simply passed through his hands on its way to the Mob.

On September 27, 2007, a federal grand jury in Chicago found three mobsters, Frank Calabrese, Sr., Joseph Lombardo, and James Marcello, guilty of killing the Spilotro brothers. Las Vegas didn't notice.

20 CHIPS AND THE WORLD
SERIES OF POKER

Today, Las Vegas is more popular than ever. The town, its history, and its culture are a revered part of the American Experience. Movies, songs, TV shows and books continue to reinforce the story that was, and still is. There is no question the death of Bugsy Siegel and the Kefauver Commission both had a significant impact on the popularity of Las Vegas. The stories of gangsters, corruption, and the Mob, all played into how Las Vegas grew and was perceived by visitors from around the globe. The casinos have even spawned a thriving subculture and community of gaming enthusiasts who collect, sell, and trade memorabilia from their favorite clubs.

Today, Bugsy Siegel, Meyer Lansky, Moe Dalitz, Wilbur Clark, and even Benny Binion remain legends of the past. The glitz, glamor, and history of Las Vegas are so compelling that photos of the past's most iconic figures now grace casino chips, and the chips themselves are collectibles!

Both the El Cortez and the Flamingo casinos are happy to align their roots to Bugsy, and his face appears on several chips. Wilbur Clark loved to see his face, so he put his photo right on the Desert Inn's chips in the 1950s. Benny Binion did the same. Their chips are now sought-after collectibles.

Binion also made an amazing contribution to the popularity of Las Vegas by hosting the World Series of Poker tournament at the Horseshoe Casino. He staged the world's biggest poker game in the 1950s between Johnny Moss and Nick Dandalos and thought up the World Series of Poker years later.

At the request of Vic Vickrey and "Amarillo Slim" Preston, he joined a group of eight poker players on a trip to Reno in 1969 to help fellow Texan Tom Moore publicize his Holiday casino. The following year, Benny and Jack Binion invited 15 top poker players to play in their own event at the Horseshoe in Las Vegas. The guys played Texas Hold'em, 5-card draw, lo-ball, and 7-stud. At the end of the week, Johnny Moss was declared the winner.

Casino players enjoyed seeing the action, and Benny decided it should be an annual event. Jimmy Snyder suggested a tournament format, and in 1971 the week-long affair ended in a Texas Hold'em freezeout tournament where six players ponied up $5,000 each to enter. Five of the players were from Texas, and four of them went on to win future WSOP tournaments. The players were Doyle Brunson, Puggy Pearson, Jack Strauss, Sailor Roberts, and Johnny Moss. Moss won the tournament.

The following year, the buy-in was raised to $10,000, when lanky and talkative "Amarillo Slim" Preston won the tournament. The press loved his country-boy charm and sense of humor so much he appeared on *The Merv Griffin Show* and *The Tonight Show with Johnny Carson.*

The WSOP was a hit, and brought poker out of the backrooms and made America see the game as one of skill, not luck. Sports Illustrated began to cover the tournament each year, as did CBS TV. The tournament's popularity increased each year, and so did the number of participants. The smiling faces of players like Doyle Brunson, Amarillo Slim, and of course their host, Benny Binion, did so much for the popularity of Las Vegas that every casino in town has profited greatly from the publicity.

Then along came online poker, and the first player to qualify online and win the Main Event, Chris Moneymaker, made players all over the world think they should come to Las Vegas and take a shot at big money. Today, the most talked about, and publicized gaming event in the world is the World Series of Poker.

Casino chips have been popular collectibles for years, but today, poker players also use collectible chips as card markers when they play. Souvenir chips, such as those made by the Gambler's General Store for the 100th Anniversary of Las Vegas in 2005 tell the story of Las Vegas, its pioneers, and the stars who came to entertain in the city. As with all collectibles, some chips are worth more than others. Chips that feature stars like Desi Arnaz or Ann-Margret sell for about $5, while those with Marilyn Monroe or Frank Sinatra sell for twice that.

Old chips from the 1950s that have Benny Binion's face on them cost a little more. The $5 chip shown earlier can be purchased for about $25. Higher denomination chips run from $40 to $100. Chips from Wilbur Clark's Desert Inn are a favorite of collectors, and even the 1950s $5 denomination chips run hundreds of dollars. The black $100 denomination chips sell for several thousand dollars. Collectors gather each year in June in Las Vegas for the Casino and Gaming Chip Show, presented by the CC&GTCC.

As for the Flamingo, the first chips produced in 1946 have a thin brass core inside, and a smooth surface sometimes called crest and seal. They were the first chips authorized by Bugsy Siegel and are very valuable to collectors. Even a chip that has been drilled and was used as a keychain sells in the neighborhood of $500. An undrilled chip commands ten times the price. Even in death, the specter of Bugsy Siegel still has a great draw on collectors and Las Vegas. It's only fitting.

That's the end, folks!

Thanks for reading *Vegas and the Mob*, I hope you enjoyed it. If you enjoyed the photos, don't be afraid to pick-up **Nevada's Golden Age of Gambling** with over 70 vintage photos from casinos all over Nevada!

Vegas and the Mob

Bibliography

Interviews for this work were done over a period of many years by the author. Those contributing significant information include:

Karl Berge, Ty Cobb, Sammy Davis, Jr., Jim Dotson, "Pick" Hobson, Johnny Moss, Warren Nelson, Sil Petricciani, Bill Pettite, Fran Pettite, Robert Ring, Harold Smith, Sr, Richard Taylor and Anthony Manzo.

Articles

Chamblin, Tony. Jimmy the Greek. Niagara Falls, New York Gambling Quarterly Spring 1974

Kerr, Robert. The Building of a Legend. Carson City, NV Nevada Magazine May/June 1985

Evans, Lance W. Rollin' With the River. Carson City, NV Nevada Magazine May/June 1991

Toll, David W. The House That Barney Built. Carson City, NV Nevada Magazine March/April 1981

Zauner, Phyllis King Karl. Carson City, NV Nevada Magazine December 1984

Richmond, Dean Reno's Brightest Corner. Reno, NV Gaming Collectors Quarterly 1994

Books

Berman, Susan. Easy Street. New York, NY The Dial Press 1981 ISBN:0-384-27185-9

Demaris, Ovid and Reid, Ed. The Green Felt Jungle. New York.

Trident Press   1963

Dietrich, Noah and Thomas, Bob. Howard. The Amazing Mr. Hughes. Greenwich, CT. Fawcett 1972

Drosnin, Michael.   Citizen Hughes.   New York, NY   Hold, Rinehart, and Winston. 1985 ISBN: 0-030041846-1

Dixon, Mead and Adams, Ken and King, R. T.   Playing the cards that are dealt.   Reno, NV   University of Nevada Oral History Program   1992 ISBN: 1-56475-365-4

Elgas, Thomas C.   Nevada Official Bicentennial Book.   Las Vegas, NV   Nevada Publications   1976

Fey, Marshall.   Slot Machines.   Las Vegas, NV   Nevada Publications   1983   ISBN: 0913814-53-9

Garrison, Omar V.   Howard Hughes in Las Vegas   New York, NY   Lyle Stuart, Inc.   1970

Jenkins, Don.   Johnny Moss-poker's Finest Champion of Champions.   Las Vegas, NV   1981

Kelley, Kitty.   His Way.   New York   Bantam Books   1986   ISBN: 0-553-26515-6

Lacey, Robert.   Little Man-Meyer Lansky And The Gangster Life. New York, NY Little Brown and Company   1991   ISBN: 0-316-51163-3

Laxalt, Robert.   Nevada: a Bicentennial history.   New York, NY W. W. Norton & Company, Inc.   1977   ISBN: 0-393005628-7

Mandel, Leon.   William Fisk Harrah.   Garden City, NY   1981 Doubleday & Company, Inc.   ISBN: 0-385-15513-1

Moehring, Eugene P.   Resort City in the Sunbelt: Las Vegas. Reno, NV   University of Nevada Press   ISBN: 0-87417-147-4

Nelson, Warren with Adams, Ken, and King, R. T. plus Nelson, Gail K.   Always Bet on the Butcher.   Reno, NV   University of Nevada Oral History Program   1994   ISBN: 1-56475-368-9

Smith, Harold S., Sr. with Noble, John Wesley.   I Want to Quit Winners.   New York Prentice-Hall, Inc.   1961

Paher, Stanley W.   Las Vegas.   Las Vegas, NV   Nevada

Publications   1971

Sawyer, Raymond I.   Reno, Where The Gamblers Go!   Reno, NV   Sawston Publishing Co.   1976

Scott, Edward B.   The Saga of Lake Tahoe, Part II.   Crystal Bay, NV   Sierra-Tahoe Publishing Co.   1973

Van Tassel, Bethel Holmes.   Wood Chips to Game Chips: Casinos and People at North Lake Tahoe.   1985

Licenses and dating from Harvey J. Fuller's Index of Nevada Gaming Establishments Harvey's Wagon Wheel, Inc.   1991

INDEX

D

E

M

N

O

P

Thanks for reading "Vegas and the Mob." You might like "Mob City: Reno" also.

CPSIA information can be obtained
at www.ICGtesting.com
Printed in the USA
LVHW020730200319
611135LV00005B/175

9 781483 955551